FROM
ROME
TO
JERUSALEM

A WANDERER'S
THOUGHTS AND
EXPERIENCES

CASLINGERLAND

SEPTEMBER 23, 1975
FEBRUARY 17, 1976

To order additional copies of this book, contact:
Xlibris
844-714-8691
www.Xlibris.com
Orders@Xlibris.com

ISBN: Softcover   978-1-5992-6419-6

Library of Congress Control Number: 2005906953

Print information available on the last page

Rev. date: 09/17/2021

TABLE OF CONTENTS

☆   ☆   ☆   ☆   ☆   ☆

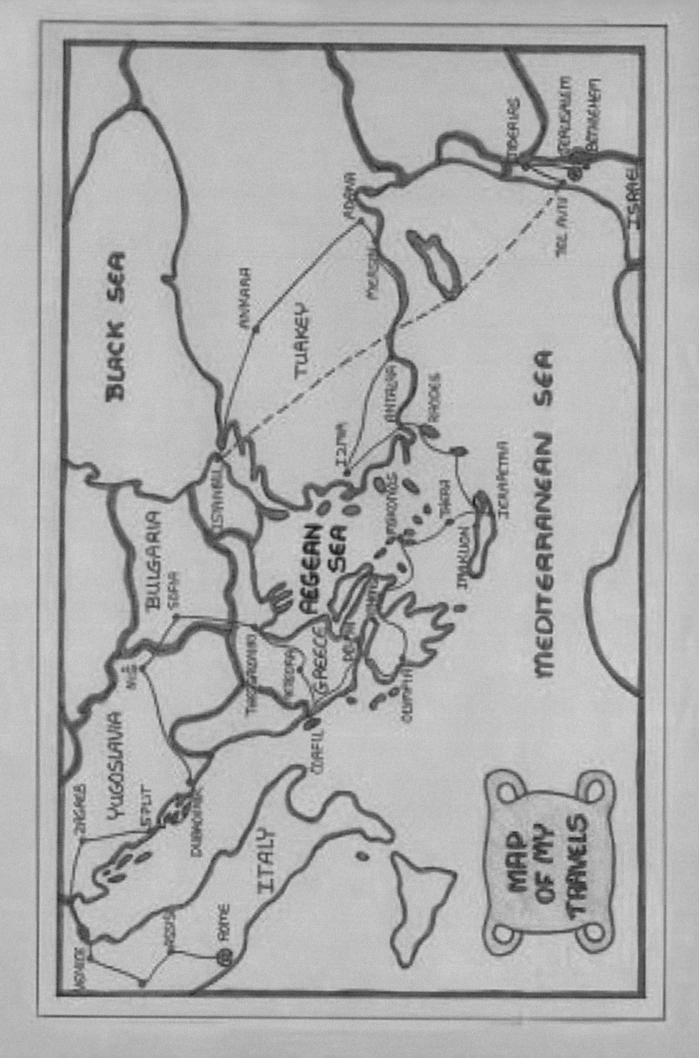

ROME ~ Sept. 23rd (Tues.) 73rd hour ~

Here I sit on the train from Naples to Rome, writing the first words of this journal as my impressions of the Sorrento Peninsula, Capri, and Pompeii slip further into the pockets of my mind. I sit with a new friend, David, a biology student from the Altos Hills, whom I met in Amalfi while waiting for the bus to Sorrento. I noticed he was reading English (*The Agony and the Ecstasy* which he had picked up in Florence) and asked him to watch my bags while I used the toilet. A friendship grew through inspiring discussions and experiences shared in Sorrento and the next day in Capri, and since Rome was the next stop for us both, we have become travelling pals for a few days. I am a loner, and prefer travelling with just my own mind but David and I share a multitude of interests and philosophies and I know that we shall cross paths again. ~ So now you shall come with me to the extent that these new impressions can spark your imagination. Enough words for now, the Italian countryside awaits my attention and the "finest" city in the world lies up the tracks an hour or so away. * Sept. 24th (Wed.) 7th hour ~

A rooster crows nearby as I woke up this morning in Rome. The search for lodging is almost forgotten now and only the satisfaction of it including remains stored and I decided to stay in the tent in a campground, a new experience for me, but only after a visit by city bus to the Youth Hostel, where David was turned away for lack of a hostel card — did we make that decision final.

DAVID

SARDINIAN CORK

KEEP ON TRUCKIN'!

Serie C   N. 254080
GRUPPO BATTELLIERI ORMEGGIATORI DI CAPRI
Via Marina Grande 196 - Capri
TRAGHETTO PER LA VISITA ALLA
GROTTA AZZURRA
LIRE 800
AUMENTO L. 75 NEI GIORNI FESTIVI

ROMA

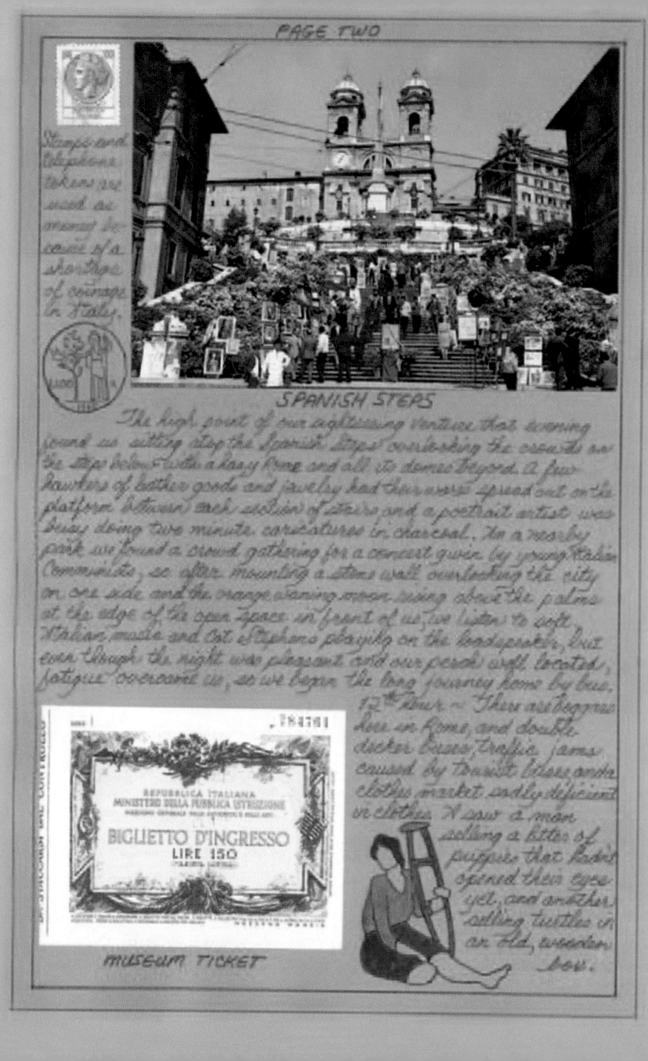

SPANISH STEPS

Stamps and telephone tokens are used as money because of a shortage of coinage in Italy.

The high point of our sightseeing venture that evening found us sitting atop the Spanish Steps overlooking the crowds on the steps below with a hazy Rome and all its domes beyond. A few hawkers of leather goods and jewelry had their wares spread out on the platform between each section of stairs and a portrait artist was busy doing two minute caricatures in charcoal. In a nearby park we found a crowd gathering for a concert given by young Italian Communists, so after mounting a stone wall overlooking the city on one side and the orange waning moon rising above the palms at the edge of the open space in front of us, we listen to soft Italian music and Cat Stephens playing on the loudspeaker, but even though the night was pleasant and our perch well located, fatigue overcame us, so we began the long journey home by bus.

12th June — There are beggars here in Rome, and double decker buses, traffic jams caused by tourists, beans and a clothes market sadly deficient in clothes. I saw a man selling a litter of puppies that hadn't opened their eyes yet, and another selling turtles in an old, wooden box.

REPUBBLICA ITALIANA
MINISTERO DELLA PUBBLICA ISTRUZIONE

BIGLIETTO D'INGRESSO
LIRE 150

MUSEUM TICKET

ATAC LIRE 50
3329
292
17709

← BUS TICKETS

⇦ PALAZZO VENEZIA

14th hour ~ I'm sitting here alongside the Palazzo Venezia while David snoozes on the rim of an abandoned fountain that's filled with broken glass, paper, and aluminium coke cans. Rome is definately not the romantic city I expected. I sort of half feel like I'm really here, even as I sit among some of the greatest monuments ever built. It's hard to close my senses to the filth and noise, to imagine the ancient grandeur. 'Ecce Homo.' 15th hour ~ David and I stand looking out over the ruins of the old Roman Forum. Our reactions were different: I was saddened at the exposure of something so beautiful to the traffic on the modern road winding thru the stately columns, walls and platforms; while David saw the tragic beauty in the strength of those columns still standing in evidence of the splendor that once was. Tourist stands sell ashtrays in the shape of the Colloseum. "It's obscene" says David. 16th hour ~ I just learned from David that marble is made from seashells that first existed in prehistoric oceans. Just think the sculptured block on which I sit is so old to begin with, but it becomes even more spiritual when you think of its age even on the day when it first felt the sculptor's chisel. 17th hour ~ Standing here on the ground level of the colloseum, I can close my eyes and imagine the Christians being torn apart by lions and close my ears to the city sounds to hear their cries and the crowds screaming for blood. They died here as martyrs and came back to build the Vatican, center of Christiandom.

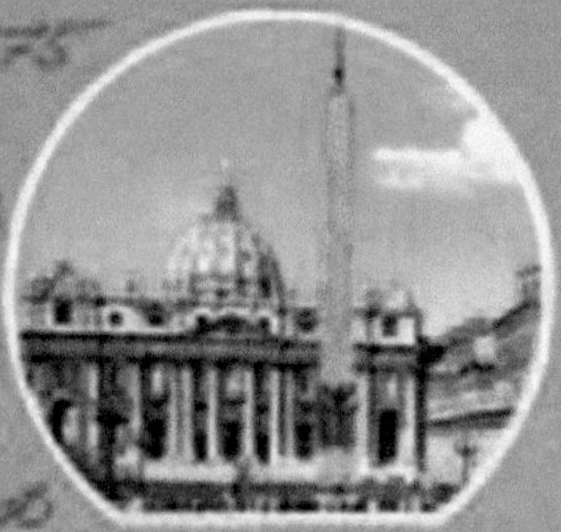

Sept. 25th (Thurs) 16th hour ~ This year of 1975 is a special one in Christiandom – the "Year of the Pilgrimage" which occurs every quarter century. Inside St Peter's Basilica, a religious group lead by monks in habits make up the greatest number of tourists. David and I watch as an old monk feebly hobbles alone towards the altar on his last pilgrimage. A singing group just entered, lead by a priest in white, holding a candle. A shaft of light cuts across my view of the altar at the far end of the nave. It's strange but, even surrounded by such things, I feel no inspiration; just seem to remember a poorly written "notice" sign at the door of a cathedral in Milan earlier this month. It read: "This cathedral is outstanding monument: holy place: it is necessary respectful behaviour and religious silence. It is not allowed to enter into cathedral to people indecently covered, unseemly to dignity to the temple of God. During the functions it is not allowed to tourist groups the visit. The parents, please keep their children." So on that final note, we shall leave Rome*

Sept. 26th (Fri) 11th hour ~ Here I stand, my big red pack resting on a baggage cart on binario (track) #2 at Orte Station, waiting to board a train to Assisi. I've just finished my second meal of the day, because now I'm starting to snack 5-6 times a day, but eating the same foods and amounts as before when I ate 3 times a day. David's with his hypoglycemia condition inspired me to do this. I have taken his address and bid him good-bye in Rome, sure that we shall meet again on my next visit to California, where he plans to have a farm. He's one of those special people in my life, someone I feel like I've always known, and no amount of time or kilometers between us can change this.

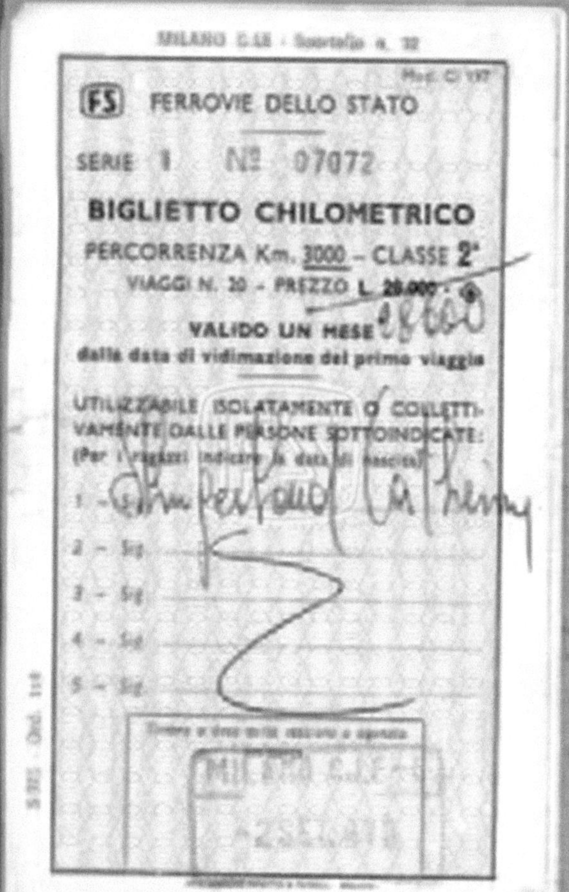

MILANO C.LE - Sportello n. 32

Mod. CI 197

FS FERROVIE DELLO STATO

SERIE 1 Nº 07072

BIGLIETTO CHILOMETRICO

PERCORRENZA Km. 3000 – CLASSE 2ª

VIAGGI N. 20 - PREZZO L. ~~20.000~~ 28.600

VALIDO UN MESE

dalla data di vidimazione del primo viaggio

UTILIZZABILE ISOLATAMENTE O COLLETTIVAMENTE DALLE PERSONE SOTTOINDICATE:

(Per i ragazzi indicare la data di nascita)

1 – Sig.

2 – Sig.

3 – Sig.

4 – Sig.

5 – Sig.

Timbro e data della stazione o agenzia

MILANO C.LE

25 SET 1975

DISCOUNT BOOK FOR ITALIAN RAIL

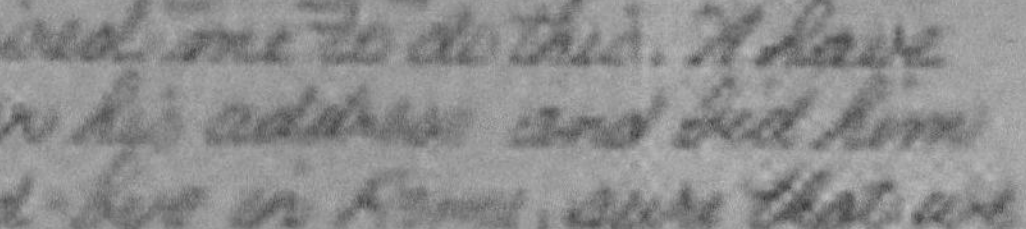

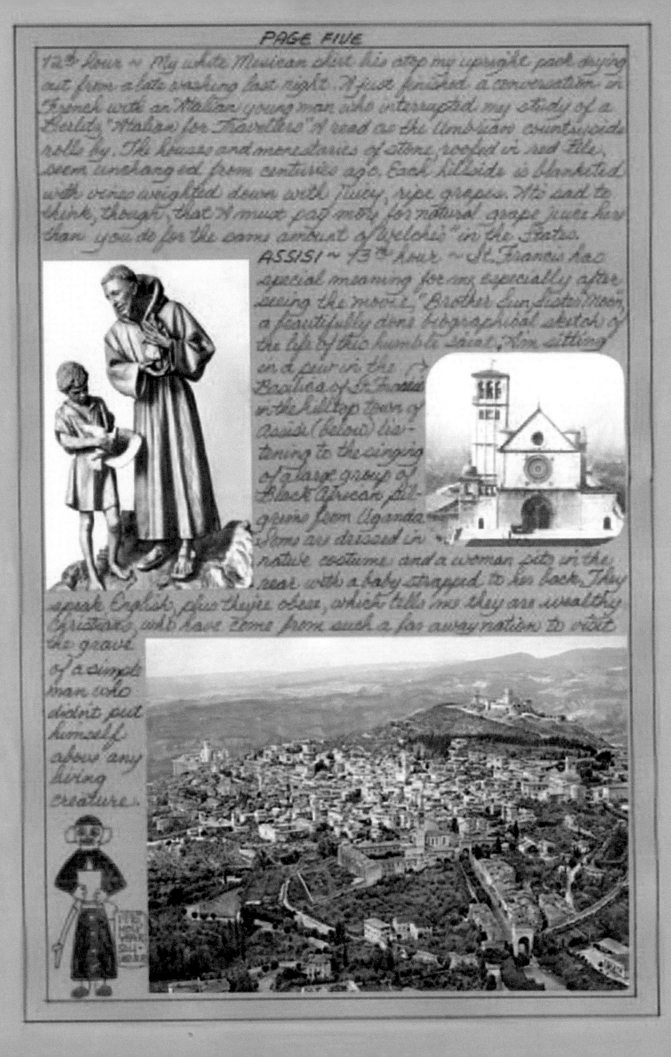

12th Hour ~ My white Mexican shirt his atop my upright pack, drying out from a late washing last night. I just finished a conversation in French with an Italian young man who interrupted my study of a Berlitz "Italian for Travellers" I read as the Umbrian countryside rolls by. The houses and monasteries of stone, roofed in red tile, seem unchanged from centuries ago. Each hillside is blanketed with vines weighted down with juicy, ripe grapes. It's sad to think, though, that I must pay more for natural grape juice here than you do for the same amount of "Welch's" in the States.

ASSISI ~ 13th hour ~ St. Francis has special meaning for me especially after seeing the movie, "Brother Sun, Sister Moon," a beautifully done biographical sketch of the life of this humble saint. I'm sitting in a pew in the Basilica of St. Francis in the hilltop town of Assisi (below) listening to the singing of a large group of Black African pilgrims from Uganda. Some are dressed in native costume and a woman sits in the rear with a baby strapped to her back. They speak English, plus they're obese, which tells me they are wealthy Christians who have come from such a far away nation to visit the grave of a simple man who didn't put himself above any living creature.

18th hour ~ I tried taking a little 'cat nap' on the train but kept thinking about a story told to David and I at the campsite in Rome. It seems that any tourist leaving Rome on a night train, is gassed and robbed in their sleep, and upon awakening, cannot find the conductor or a sympathetic policeman. They say all roads lead to Rome, well I'm glad they also lead away and also I'm on one of them. ✳ ✳ ✳

SEPT. 27th (Sz.) 3rd hour ~ I just woke up after four broken hours of sleep, ate a few dried figs, and contemplated if I should use the "gabinetti" toilet, now or on the 4:14 train to Padua. Decided 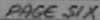 ←ME

to write a few words as I sit here in the second class waiting room of the station in Florence. My train from David arrived late so I missed the connection which would have allowed me twenty minutes to change trains. One must accept things like this when travelling, and see changes in plans as challenges to one's wisdom and endurance. I'm lucky that this is a relatively clean, well lit and crowded waiting room. I cannot say so much for the Italian cities further south. There's an old burn behind me and one beside me, but it makes no difference any more; travelling cuts down class barriers and I know we all live in the same world.

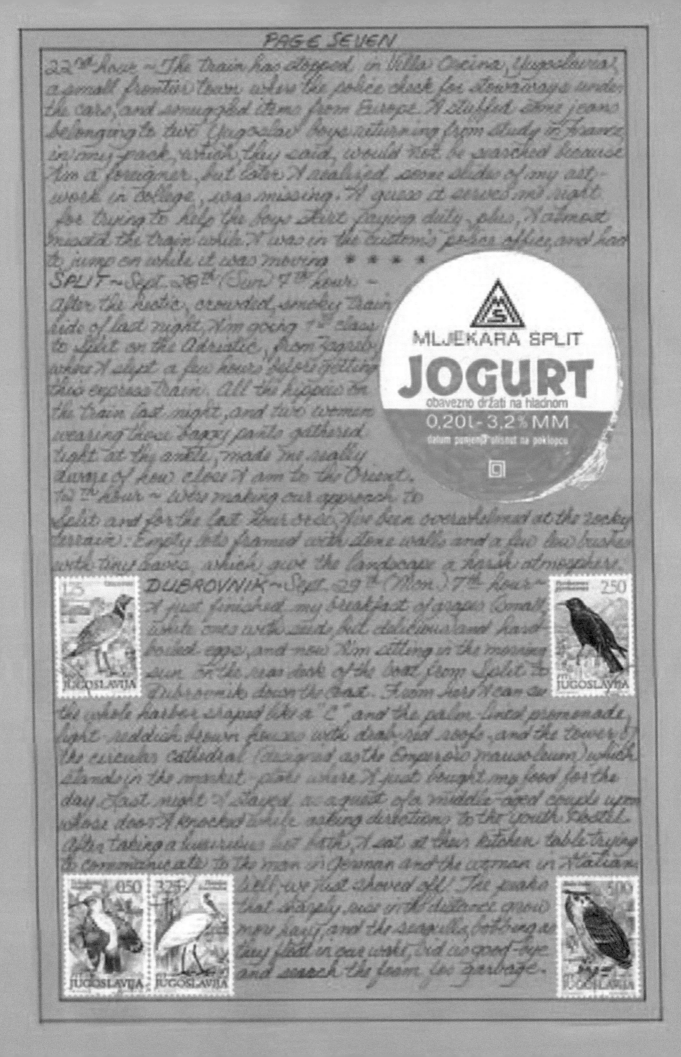

22ⁿᵈ hour ~ The train has stopped in Villa Oscina, Yugoslavia, a small frontier town where the police check for stowaways under the cars, and smuggled items from Europe. A stuffed store jeans belonging to two Yugoslav boys returning from study in France, in my pack, which they said, would not be searched because I'm a foreigner, but later I realized some slides of my art-work in college, was missing. A guess it serves me right for trying to help the boys skirt paying duty, plus, I almost missed the train while I was in the custom's police office, and had to jump on while it was moving * * * * *

SPLIT ~ Sept. 28ᵗʰ (Sun) 7ᵗʰ hour ~ After the hectic, crowded, smokey train ride of last night, I'm going 1ˢᵗ class to Split on the Adriatic, from Zagreb where I slept a few hours before getting this express train. All the hippies on the train last night, and two women wearing these baggy pants gathered tight at the ankle, made me really aware of how close I am to the Orient.

14ᵗʰ hour ~ We're making our approach to Split and for the last hour or so I've been overwhelmed at the rocky terrain: Empty lots framed with stone walls and a few low bushes with tiny leaves, which give the landscape a harsh atmosphere.

DUBROVNIK ~ Sept. 29ᵗʰ Mon. 7ᵗʰ hour ~ I just finished my breakfast of grapes (small white ones with seeds but delicious) and hard-boiled eggs, and now I'm sitting in the morning sun on the rear deck of the boat from Split to Dubrovnik down the coast. From here I can see the whole harbor shaped like a "C" and the palm-lined promenade, light-reddish-brown houses with drab-red roofs, and the tower of the circular cathedral (designed as the Emperor's mausoleum) which stands in the market-place where I just bought my food for the day. Last night I stayed in a quiet of a middle-aged couple upon whose door I knocked while asking directions to the youth hostel. After taking a luxurious hot bath, I sat at their kitchen table trying to communicate to the man in German and the woman in Italian. Well, we just showed off! The snow-capped mountains that sharply rise in the distance grow more hazy, and the seagulls, bobbing as they float in our wake, bid us good-bye and snatch the food, we garbage.

20th hour ~ The crowds are still pouring in and taking their seats for the folklore show here atop the old stone fort, part of the "Old City" of Dubrovnik. From my seat I look down upon the small harbor, many tiny boats resting on its semi-lit water, and the walls and towers still standing despite the earthquake of 1667, stretch 2.5 kms. to enclose the narrow streets, Rector's Palace, Cathedral of St. Biagio, and Franciscan Monastery. A young man of 21 years, Felix, whom I met on the ferry, is one of the dancers, and because of his gentlemanly nature, quite rare for Mediterranean boys his age, he has become my companion. A music student now, but after graduation, he wants to travel, so will probably crew a ship to learn navigation.

23rd hour ~ The show, even though it lasted 3 hours, was captivating: the dancers made some quite strenuous and fleet moves, sometimes stamping hard to a downbeat and other times flicking the lower leg with a unique twist to the ankle. The rapid circular movements of the whole group at times reminded me of the cup-and-saucer ride at a carnival when seen at a distance. Well, it's been a long day and I'm ready for a good night's sleep, for a change, here, in my first room rented in Yugoslavia: a clean room in a woman's house, conveniently located, for which I pay under $3.

⇦ OPEN MARKET IN THE OLD CITY

* * * * *

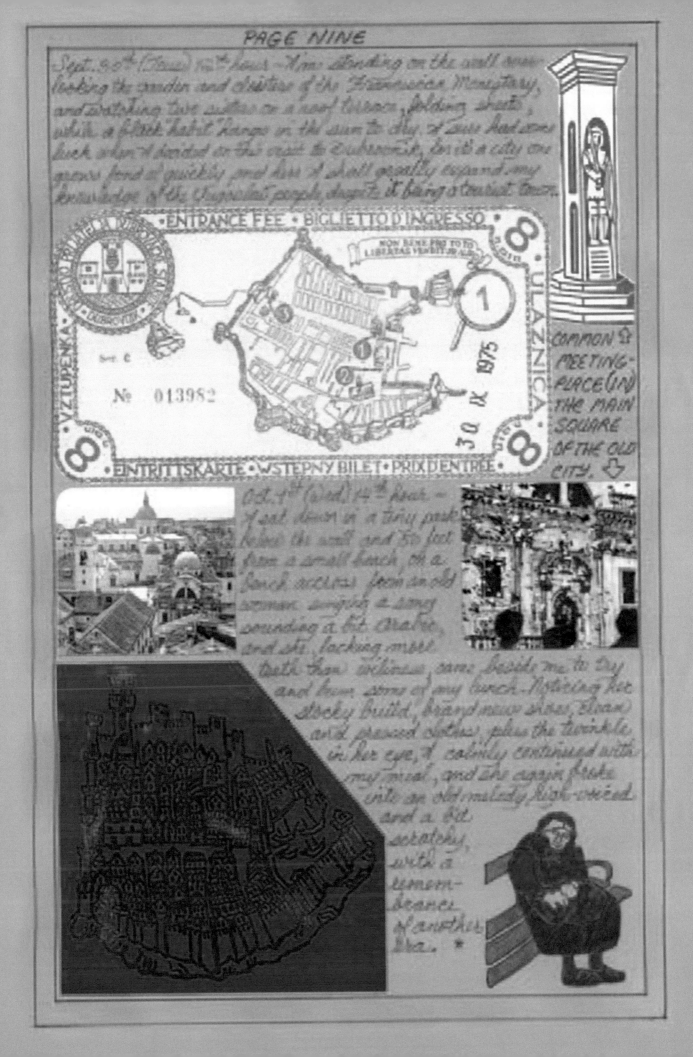

Sept. 30th (Tues) 12th hour — Here standing on the wall near looking the garden and cloisters of the Franciscan Monastery, and watching two sisters on a roof terrace, folding sheets, while a black habit hangs in the sun to dry. I sure had some luck when I decided on this visit to Dubrovnik, for it's a city one grows fond of quickly, and here I shall greatly expand my knowledge of the Yugoslav people, despite it being a tourist town.

ENTRANCE FEE · BIGLIETTO D'INGRESSO ·
ULAZNICA
VZTUPENKA
No 013982
30 IX 1975
ENTRITTSKARTE · WSTEPNY BILET · PRIX D'ENTREE

COMMON MEETING-PLACE (IN) THE MAIN SQUARE OF THE OLD CITY.

Oct. 1st (Wed.) 14th hour — I sat down in a tiny park below the wall and 50 feet from a small bench, on a bench across from an old woman, singing a song sounding a bit Arabic, and she, lacking more teeth than wrinkles, came beside me to try and bum some of my lunch. Noticing her stocky build, brand new shoes, clean and pressed clothes, plus the twinkle in her eye, I calmly continued with my meal, and she again broke into an old melody, high-voiced and a bit scratchy, with a remembrance of another era. *

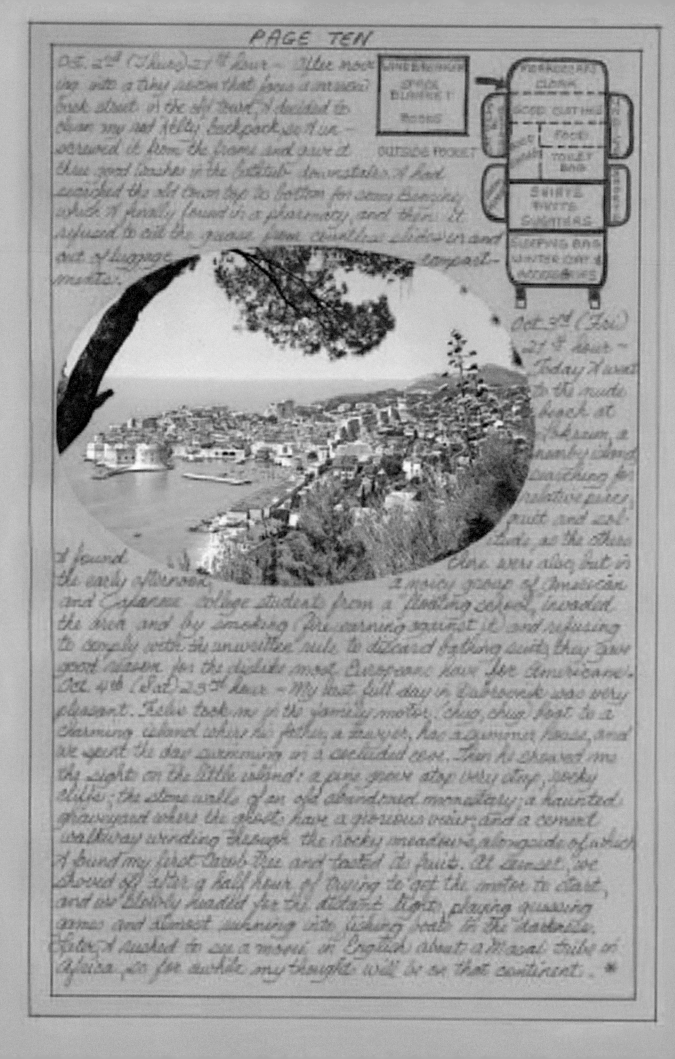

Oct. 2nd (Thurs) 27th hour — After noon nap, into a tiny room that faced a mussed fresh street in the off-hours, I decided to clean my rest (Kelty) backpack, so I un-screwed it from the frame and gave it three good washes in the bathtub downstairs. I had searched the old town top to bottom for some Benzine, which I finally found in a pharmacy, and then it refused to oil the queue from cruiseless sliders in and out of luggage compart-ments.

Oct. 3rd (Fri) 27th hour — Today I went to the nudist beach at Sveti Jakov, a nearby island, searching for meditative peace, quiet and solitude, as the others there were alike, but in the early afternoon, a noisy group of American and Japanese college students from a "floating school," invaded the area and by smoking (the warning against it) and refusing to comply with its unwritten rule to discard bathing suits they gave good reason for the dislike most Europeans have for Americans.

Oct. 4th (Sat) 29th hour — My last full day in Dubrovnik was very pleasant. Felix took me in the family motor, "chug, chug, boat to a charming island where his father, a lawyer, has a summer house, and we spent the day swimming in a secluded cove. Then he showed me the sights on the little island: a pine grove atop very steep, rocky cliffs; the stone walls of an old abandoned monastery; a haunted graveyard where the ghosts have a glorious view; and a cement walkway winding through the rocky meadows, alongside of which I found my first Carob tree and tasted its fruits. At sunset, we shoved off after a half hour of trying to get the motor to start, and we blindly headed for the distant light, playing guessing games and almost running into fishing boats in the darkness. Later, I rushed to see a movie, in English about a Masai tribe in Africa, so for awhile my thoughts will be on that continent. *

NIŠ - Oct. 6th (Mon) 9th hour - I'm sitting feeling a bit stranded here in the bus station at Niš, the finish of my long trek through Yugoslavia, where the most memorable part of the trip was the treacherous climb on a narrow hairpinned road from a scenic inlet to the panoramic view of the cliffs high above, in an area south of Dubrovnik. Now I must endure a nine-hour wait before my trip to Sofia, and who knows what I may find there? It's a good time to share my observations of the Yugoslav people. The country is not so scary as I thought in the beginning, but was under Turkish rule for a long time, accounting for the Arabic-sounding language (Serbo-Croat), and the simple-mindedness and aggressive nature of the people. They are basically peasant types: Slavic, with flat, round faces, light features, thin lips and round noses; or Arabic, with thin lips also, but dark and with sharp, thinner features. Their character is nervous and quite pushy. Some of the younger are of a more gentle nature, with refined, more intelligent features, but even this is rare, for when they are in a group, they become a little savages, always with an apathetic nature and lack of respect for strangers. Sometimes when asked a very simple thing, they act dumb, and in such a way that it seems they don't know who or where they are. All the men and some women smoke cigarettes, and are quite ignorant of rules of health and nutrition. As long as I stay in a tourist place like Dubrovnik, where I was invited by Felicia's father to return and stay in the summer house, I will always find people who speak English, but here they don't even know the word "toilet."

12th hour - Sitting here for so long has given me a good chance to observe the clothing of the people. Those who could fit without notice into a Western European city life, wear the fashions of a decade ago, but the majority look as if they're wearing all the clothing they own. The old women and some of the married young women wear black or dark-colored midi-skirts, shirts, sweaters, scarfs, stockings and black slippers (sometimes bedroom slippers) some being rubber with one strap. It's pepper (paprika) season, and I notice a few women lugging plastic and net bags, and scarfs filled with peppers, coming or going between farm and market. The older men wear the same rubber shoes, but mostly tied black shoes, dark trousers, thick sweaters, vests (sometimes leather), Kossuth hats, taxi driver caps, or "acrylic-top" hats. Only the young women wear pants, rarely tight, and the young men wear jeans and conservative shirts, sweaters and jackets of brighter colors. I seem to be the only Westerner here. *

SOFIA ~ Oct. 7th ~ (and 19th hour ~ Well, it is the end of my one day in this city and you are probably quite anxious to hear what life is like in Bulgaria. I certainly felt the influence of communism in the air (along with the smell of dead leaves) which overwhelmed me with nostalgia, a feeling I must control here, worlds away from the streets, yards, fields, and woods of my childhood. Has this influence made the people colder, better, safer, or unfriendly? Going by my experience from the border last night to the youth hostel where I am now, I have met some of the most friendly, kind and helpful people on my trip, and they often go out of their way or take the time to guide me to a certain place or give me what I need. At the start of my leisurely walk this morn-

ing, I visited the Tomonova train station, still under construction, and was impressed by the large modern relief which ran the full length of the main wall in-side. It followed a bulky, geome-trical style I've seen before in the

Russian pavilions at world's fairs and which I saw repeated in signs, posters and statues. Even Biblical scenes painted on the walls of a church had a hard-edged, planular quality. The largest indoor supermarket where I decided to do a little shopping and observing, I found very neat and extremely well organized, but oddly deficient in fresh fruits and vegetables. The variety and supply of canned goods and fruit juices is excellent however, and the whole containing of seemingly the same brand throughout the store, look as if they come straight from some canning factory on a farm cooperative outside the city. Except for some English tea I saw, nothing is imported, and I didn't notice bananas being sold anywhere, or fruit other than lemons, apples and a few grapes. All the housewives buy fresh produce in huge quantities, probably for home canning of seasonal foods. The center of the city is conveniently small, and yet doesn't have a confused, rushed, or closed-in feeling, partly because cars are so expensive, and half the streets are barren. I decided to spend the afternoon in the reading room of the American Embassy, but after listening to childish conversations in that "gnawing" accent, I was glad to be in foreign lands.

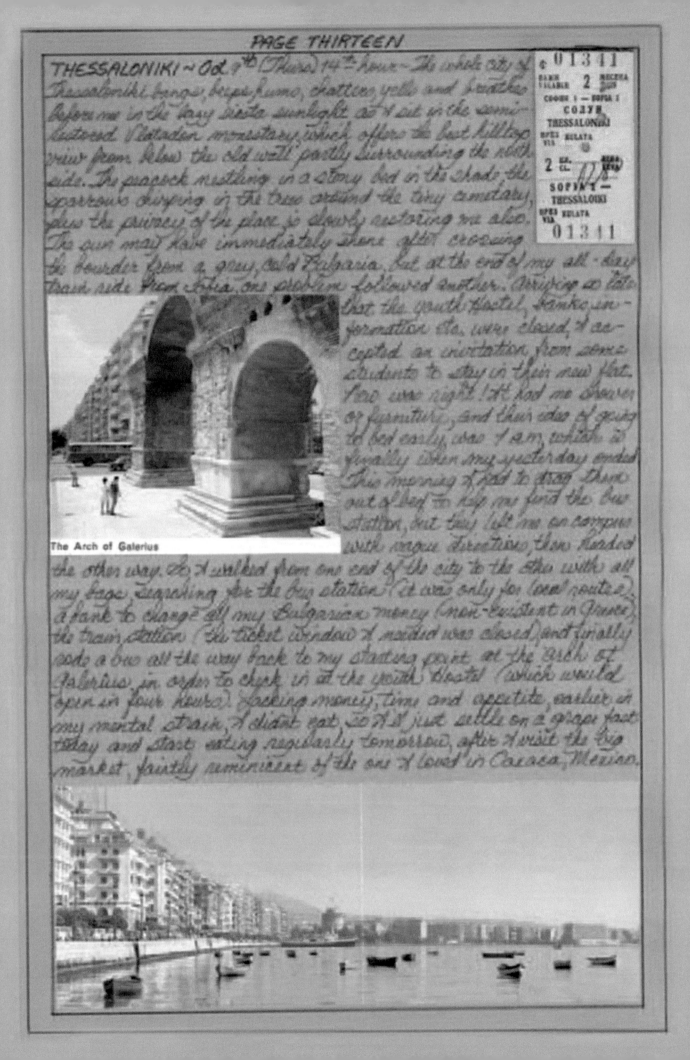

THESSALONIKI ~ Oct. 9th (Thurs) 14th hour ~ The whole city of Thessaloniki bangs, beeps, hums, chatters, yells and breathes before me in the hazy siesta sunlight as I sit in the semi-restored Vlatadon monastery, which offers the best hilltop view from below the old wall partly surrounding the north side. The peacock nestling in a stony bed in the shade, the sparrows chirping in the tree around the tiny cemetary, plus the privacy of the place, is slowly restoring me also. The sun may have immediately shone after crossing the bourder from a grey, cold Bulgaria, but at the end of my all-day train ride from Sofia, one problem followed another. Arriving so late that the youth hostel, banks, information etc. were closed, I ac-cepted an invitation from some students to stay in their new flat. Here was night! It had no shower or furniture, and their idea of going to bed early was 1 a.m., which is finally when my yesterday ended. This morning I had to drag them out of bed to help me find the bus station, but they led me on campus with vague directions, then headed the other way. So, I walked from one end of the city to the other with all my bags, searching for the bus station (it was only for local routes), a bank to change all my Bulgarian money (non-existent in Greece), the train station (the ticket window I needed was closed,) and finally rode a bus all the way back to my starting point at the Arch of Galerius, in order to check in at the youth hostel (which would open in four hours). Lacking money, time and appetite, earlier in my mental strain, I didn't eat. So I'll just settle on a grape fast today and start eating regularly tomorrow, after I visit the big market, faintly reminiscent of the one I loved in Oaxaca, Mexico.

The Arch of Galerius

Oct 20th (Fri) 9th hour— The sky was still black and oozes of rain formed puddles in the streets of Thessaloniki, and in my pre-dawn awakening I felt a new rush of excitement. It's wonderful to walk the streets when only magazine stand and bar owners are preparing for business in the dawn light. I am in high so lift and when I lean out of the window of this speeding train, and the world of nature and pockets of civilization fly by, I project my mind into that world which has no other name but "Planet Earth," and forget that the wind is tangling my hair and that behind me are smoke-filled, crowded cabins. The smell of fresh pastry in the dining car already reaches my nose, reminding me of the bakery at the "Four Seasons" where Aunt Kay took us children to get those big almond sugar cookies with red jelly in the center, and sometimes the very same smoke comes to remind me of a ski-lift amusement, and standing at the bottom of a snowy slope anticipating the downhill run, thinking of how to improve my style. I think on things so distant, so remote, because with all the miles between me and my origins, I must take my home with me, in my mind, and this ever X-day gathering, and growing inside, viewing each new foreign as just a new corner of my backyard, a place that will become easily familiar with passing time. Time I have forgotten what this is. I know that I am heading for the Acropolis in Athens by the full moon, but when I make these rare studies of myself in the mirror, I have not aged but grown younger. An old woman with her turkeys and a long pole that she waves threateningly at the train, the shepherd tending black and white flocks of sheep that run from the thundering "iron horse"— they have no time. Chickens scratch the dry ground while pigs copulate in the pens as the train speeds and scarecrows stand in the lonely cornfields getting more tattered year after year. Year? What year? The year when I turned 25, yet I am but a child, a child of Nature, of Man, of Divine Thought.

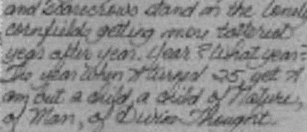

12th hour ~ Oh, what a thrill to change onto a ricketty little train that grinds its way through the northern Greek countryside, a sight made up mostly of ripe cotton fields, gardens irrigated according to the imaginations of the individual farmers, and countless small yards, one filled with geese, another occupied by a single old swaybacked horse ready for the glue factory, and still another containing a little dog surveying his territory from the back of a spotted cow lying down there on the sun-baked dirt.

Trikala

19th Hour – The echoes of sheep and goat bells far below, and the deep barking a "good night" to their friends in the valley, air carried up to me through the gorges and caprices, by the cool moist wind in this sunset hour, but the peace is shaken abruptly by the drum beat "tapal" of the ten monks in the monastery "Great Meteora," perched upon the largest mass of towering rock across a ravine about 500 feet from where I sit atop another pinnacle. One by one the lights go out in the north-west section of the centuries-old holy place of hermits, but I have only the glow of the waning crescent moon, trying to pierce the clouds which add to the eerie feeling of the place. I sense, as I sit on this rock (as if on Olympus, home of the gods) that I share the spirit with the spirits of the hermits of the ages past, gentle souls who fled civilization to live a life of solitude in preparation for a higher spiritual existence. Tonight, I shall also sleep under a rock overhang as they did, and awaken before the sun, alone with nature, the divine spirits of the holy men, and the gods. ✳ ✳ ✳ ✳

THE HOLY MONASTERY OF THE GREAT METEORON

Frescoes-Monastery of Varlaam

Oct. 14th Cloud 9th hour~
Writing a few notes for
this book is an excellent
way to pass the time on
these ferries which I am
using more now that I
am in Greece. This morn-
ing I'm about to leave
Corfu, where I spent two
nights in Corfu Town,
having explored the mar-
ket and tourist shops
which abound on the
numerous and narrow

⇧ IGOUMENITSA

"Venetian" streets and alleyways, plus a bit of the countryside,
thanks to two Greek fellows, partners in a small real estate
business, and a couple of American gals, teen ebattle who added
to the fun of yesterday afternoon's drive to a monastery, scenic
cliffs and isolated from roads. I shall now return to Igoumenitsa across the bay where I already stayed one night, and
then catch the bus for Delphi.   *   *   CORFU COAST ⇩

DELPHI ~ Oct. 16 (Thurs) 10th hour.
Sometimes I just can't get inspired to write, as was the case these past few days when I travelled all the way from Corfu to Delphi, spending 2 nights in the youth hostel there, then on to Patras, where I sat in the train / bus / ferry station waiting for my train to Olympia. The only memorable part of the trip, which was the sunset before arriving in Corfu, and then at my first glimpse of Delphi, I was taken aback by the lit up, touristy main street, lined with shops of furs, hats and coats (a speciality in central Greece) re-plicas of ancient Greek pottery, woolen shawls and blankets and hand embroidered shirts and dresses. I was also a bit surprised to see most of the signs written in Greek plus English, and all the tour groups plus young European and American backpackers hanging out all over.

However, my main purpose, of course, was to see the ancient and archaeological arsenal this place deemed to be "the centre of the Earth." I was deeply impressed by the fact that long ago, rich and poor alike, came to this very spot, and, despite the fact that all the beautiful buildings have crumbled down with fierce earthquakes and erosion, I feel quite at home here. The place still holds an aura of divinity and those who live in Delphi be- lieve that the gods are still there.

TICKET FROM THE DELPHI RUINS ☞

474416 ΕΙΣΙΤΗΡΙΟΝ
ΔΕΛΦΟΙ | ΜΟΥΣΕΙΟΝ - ΙΕΡΟΝ ΔΡ DR 30

15 OCT 1974

DELFI

Apollo, son of Olympian Zeus, was not originally worshipped at the spot where his most famous oracle was later established. During the movements of tribes around the end of the second and the beginning of the first millennium, he came either from the north or from Dorian Kriti to this place which was then known as Pytho.

He came to this spot where the cliffs of Parnassos are bathed in light, where they rise up sheer to heaven. Down below is the deep valley of Plistos which opens up into the Plain of Kirra with its cloak of olive trees.

Beyond the plain gleams the Corinthian Gulf and the high mountains of the northern Peloponnissos lie blue on the horizon. The sanctuary lies in a fold of the hill formed by the Fedriades, two enormous grey rocks whose peaks rise up like towers over the landscape and cast a mystical light over the ruins. Behind these towers the mountain wall of Kirphis, and the whole area has an almost dream-like atmosphere as the harsh light is reflected between the two red rocks, Rodini and Flembouko.

The unique grandeur of the landscape makes you feel the uniqueness of the god who was worshipped here long before Apollo came. It is said that at the end of the 2nd millennium, Mother Earth was still worshipped in the opening from which the Kastalia Spring gushed out.

The people of Delfi developed into an autonomous state governed by the noble families who guarded the autonomy and the wealth of the sanctuary.

The sanctuary became the centre of a religious federation the Amphiktyonian League, which was composed of 12 members, all neighbouring cities. It had more or less the same objects as a similar modern League of Nations, the union of city states with common religious, political and commercial interest.

TEMPLE OF APOLLO

THE NAVEL

The ancients believed that Delfi was the centre of the earth, the point of contact between this world and God, the navel of the earth, the place where two eagles met after being loosed by Zeus in different directions to indicate the centre of the earth.

In the Greek mind, the God Apollo embodies moral discipline and purity of spirit and the oracle at Delfi was the first to put forward the idea of forgiveness of sin, the liberation of slaves by gods, and the equality of rich and poor before God.

The Sanctuary of Apollo, the heart of Delfi, is on the southern edge of the mountain slope, a little above the road which comes from Arahova. It forms a square. Beginning from the southeastern edge, the Sacred Way winds snake-like up the mountain flanked by treasuries and state monuments up to the remains of the large Doric temple of Apollo which dominates the sanctuary. Here was the seat of the oracle, an underground vault where the Pythia, sitting on a tripod, pronounced her oracular sayings, which the priests wrote down and recited as counsels of the god. After a conflagration in 548 B.C. the temple was rebuilt on a grander scale with elaborate pediments and it now enclosed the crypt and the inner sanctuary with the laurel. The remains we see today are of the 4th century temple that was rebuilt after an earthquake. Written on the walls of the temple are sayings of wise men of Greece: "Know thyself", "Moderation in all things" and so on.

OLYMPIA

TEMPLE OF ZEUS

This cult of beauty and physical strength had its beginnings in the first millenium B.C., when the Elians, thought to have arrived from the north, settled close to this region and most probably dedicated it to Zeus, naming it Olympia in memory of Mt. Olympos in Thessalia.

The first festivals celebrated in Olympia were given in honour of the mythical King Pelops, after whom Peloponisos is named. Pelops, so the legend goes, defeated Oinomaos,

king of neighbouring Pisa, in a chariot race and then married his daughter, Hippodamia. In later years the Olympic Games and Festival were established in honour of Zeus, and the first games were contested between gods and heroes.

Historically however, the Games began in 776 B.C., and were for some ten centuries milestones of time. "That was the year", a Greek would say when talking of some past event, "when Philippides won the pentathlon". From 776 B.C. to 393 A.D. this pagan festival was celebrated with reason and good will every four years, until the zeal of a Christian emperor decided to suppress it.

The Original Olympics were not only an athletic and religious event. In the evenings, after the games were over, men and minds met to discuss philosophy, to compete in song and music, to feast, and even to make treaties. A record of every victor in each Olympiad since 776 B.C. still exists.

In 676 B.C., the Games took on a panhellenic character, culminating with the Sacred Truce, signed in 576 B.C. This vow of peace entailed the suspension of all hostilities for one month, called the "Hierominia", or holy month, so that warriors too could participate in the Games.

The Games themselves lasted for five days, starting on the first day of the midsummer full moon. Athletes from all parts of the Greek world arrived at Olympia to take part in such events as the foot races, wrestling, jumping, discus and javelin throwing, chariot and horse races. By custom the victorious athlete was crowned with the Olympic wreath of wild olive – the highest honour a Greek could win.

With the advent of Christianity social and religious aspirations eventually brought about radical changes and the monuments of the old, pagan religion were used to provide stones for the construction of a castle and bastion of the new faith. Finally, in 393 A.D., Theodosius I decreed the Games unlawful, and Theodosius II ordered the total destruction of the sanctuary some time after that. The death blow to Olympia's faded glory was delivered by Alaric and the invading Goths. In the 6th century A.D. the last semblance of Olympia's glorious past was annihilated by earthquakes, and in the succeeding centuries the flooding of Alfios gently buried the ancient ground, piously leaving the sacred grove untouched.

It was not until 1875 that systematic archaeological excavation once again brought Olympia to light. The Modern Olympic Games were revived in 1896 by a French sportsman, Baron de Coubertin, and have since been held every four years, each Olympiad in a different country, and participated in by athletes the world over.

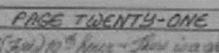

OLYMPIA~ Oct. 17 (Wed) 10ᵗʰ piece ~ There is a group of German tourists standing at the entrance of the stadium, and for a joke, one middle-aged man took off his shirt and ran to the far end and back, returning to a few hands clapping amidst laughter, the sound drifting away in the morning breeze. But when I entered earlier under the arch, and threw the passage away to the long empty field, it could hear in my mind the crowds cheering from the sloping, grassy sides, now only occupied by foraging magpies, and A raised my arms in a Champion's handclasp, ran halfway down the field to Demeter's altar, a small stone platform, and climbed atop it where I sit now, thinking of ages past.

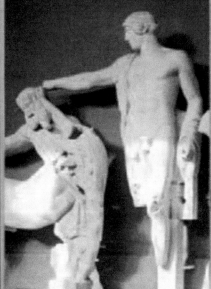

All who enter the Olympiad in these times, should make a visit here to be inspired to perform in the original consciousness instead of the business it's turned into. It can be a very rewarding experience to walk among ancient ruins like this, but saddening too, for A want so much to go back in time and become a part of Olympia, or any other ruined site, just to know what it was like to live there, wearing the clothes, walking the streets and garden paths, eating and talking with friends. Well, the entrance of a boisterous group of young Greeks, preparing for a footrace, is my cue to return to the pine-treed paths through broken columns, walls, and dreams. #

ATHENS ~ Oct. 18 (Sat) 22nd hour ~ It is a very rare, precious moment in my travels as I write these words; the full moon is my lamp, sitting on a marble block at the foot of the Parthenon atop the Acropolis, surrounded completely by the light of modern Athens below. The brief showers of the sunset hour threatened to drench this evening but I had planned for, but I bumped into a tour director who guided me to a special engraving of the "Sound and Light Show" which doesn't usually play during the three or four nights of the full moon, and seconds before the music sounded to our anxious ears, the moon in all her bright glory shone forth from behind the clouds billowing by, accompanied by Venus, also shining brightly. After the inspiring show I hurried from the Pnyx Hill to the Acropolis which remains open on nights of the full moon, to marvel at the silvery columns of stone reaching up to the heavens. The moon suddenly encircled herself with a multicolored halo of light — a rainbow; something which I have never before seen. * * * * *

Oct. 22nd (Wed) 6th hour ~
Well, I'm shoving off again,
this time from Piraeus, leaving
Athens to awaken beneath a
fluorescent gold, pink-orange
and yellow-blue sky with the
sun's rays shafting from
billowing clouds, and after
five nights, it is difficult
to leave this city that I would
prefer to live in over all the
other large, capital cities I
have visited so far.

A 2267544
ΑΚΡΟΠΟΛΙΣ
ΕΙΣΙΤΗΡΙΟΝ
ΔΡΧ 30

The byzantine church of Agii Theodori

ΕΛΛΑΣ HELLAS

Athens is not so dangerous
that I always had to be on
guard because the Greeks,
even in the big city, are
quite friendly, and thanks
to the tour attractor, I saw
the Acropolis Museum plus
another one, two churches,
a suburb filled with
gorgeous homes that you would all
appreciate, the yachting harbour near
a ruined church where St. Paul taught,
the rocky shore of the Attiki Peninsula,
the marble quarry and panoramic
views of Athens from surrounding cliffs.

I even saw a good share of films in English, plus a few cartoons, the ones I remember from my younger years, before they started making those cheap ones the children watch today in the States. Speaking of children, I'm finding the Greek mentality to be quite childish, and with their fears and lack of healthy habits, they look five to twenty years older than they should. Off they continue apathetically with their old ways, not caring about the consequences in old age, when all of them can be seen limping, coughing, quitting, and huffing and puffing as they carry their mounds of fat around, marvelling at the heavy pack on my back, not thinking that they're carrying the same extra twenty kilos which can't be shed so easily. There is not so much concern about proper waste disposal, and the landscapes, streets and shores look it. As far as plumbing and sanitation are concerned, hot showers are rare, and I sometimes don't need to read the signs to sense where the toilets are, most of which are the Arabic kind with just a hole in the floor (they seldom flush either). But Greece, caught between the East and West, is still my favorite country so far, because it's not too civilized nor too primitive, and being in Athens, I was given a chance to catch up with the world, before heading for the simpler life on the islands, where I plan to work if the weather and tourist population permit * *

Owner Publisher and Managing Editor
YANNIS HORN 19 Lassou Street
Chief Printer: DAFLIS 138 Acadimias Street

Telephones

Athens News

Daily in English

GREECE: Three months drs 300. six months drs 1200. one year 2200.
EUROPE: Seasurface Mail
Three months
Six months
One year

Air Mail

MID-EAST
Air Mail one year
Cyprus-Egypt: One year

Here are some words which you are bound to need during your short stay in Greece.		
Parakalo — Please	*Thio* — Two	*Estiatorio* — Restaurant
Kalimera — Good morning	*Tria* — Three	*Taxithi* — Travel
Poso kani — How much does it cost?	*Tessera* — Four	*Praktorio* — Agency
To logariasmo — The bill	*Pende* — Five	*Ipothromos* — Race course
Aposkeves — The luggage	*Exi* — Six	*Anikto* — Open
Pou ine? — Where is it?	*Epta* — Seven	*Klisto* — Closed
Epano — Upstairs	*Okto* — Eight	*Ti ora ine* — What time is it?
Kato — Downstairs	*Enea* — Nine	*Simera* — Today
Eki — There	*Theka* — Ten	*Avrio* — Tomorrow
Etho — Here	*Efharisto* — Thank you	*Andio* — Good bye
Thexia — Right	*Pote* — When	*Hthes* — Yesterday
Aristera — Left	*Gramatosimo* — Stamp	*Proi* — Morning
Nero — Water	*Limani* — Port	*Apoyevma* — Afternoon
Zesto nero — Hot water	*Plio* — Ship	*Vrathi* — Evening
Thomatio — Room	*Treno* — Train	*Imera* — Day
Gramma — Letter	*Stathmos* — Station	*Nichta* — Night
Presvia — Embassy	*Aerothromio* — Airport	*Minas* — Month
Telonio — Customs house	*Leoforio* — Bus	*Evthomas* — Week
Ena — One	*Thromos* — Street, way	*Thelo* — I want
	Katastima — Shop	*Kalo* — Good
	Yatros — Doctor	*Kako* — Bad
	Farmakio — Drugstore	*Epistrepo* — Permitted
	Nosokomio — Hospital	*Fevgo* — I am leaving

Oct. 23rd (Thurs) 11th hour - This morning as I was descending the outer stairway of the house where I slept last night, who should I meet first, but Mr. Pink Pelican, slowly waddling his scratchy pigeon-toed (sorry friend) webbed-foot way through the white-arched alleys of tiny Mykonos. I was forced to play follow-the-leader for a short distance until the path divided, but later saw him with his undyed friend, quite a naughty fellow, and a few cats, down where the fishermen dock their boats to sell their bounty from the sea.   MYKONOS

SQUID, A DELICASY, HANGING TO DRY. ⤵

69

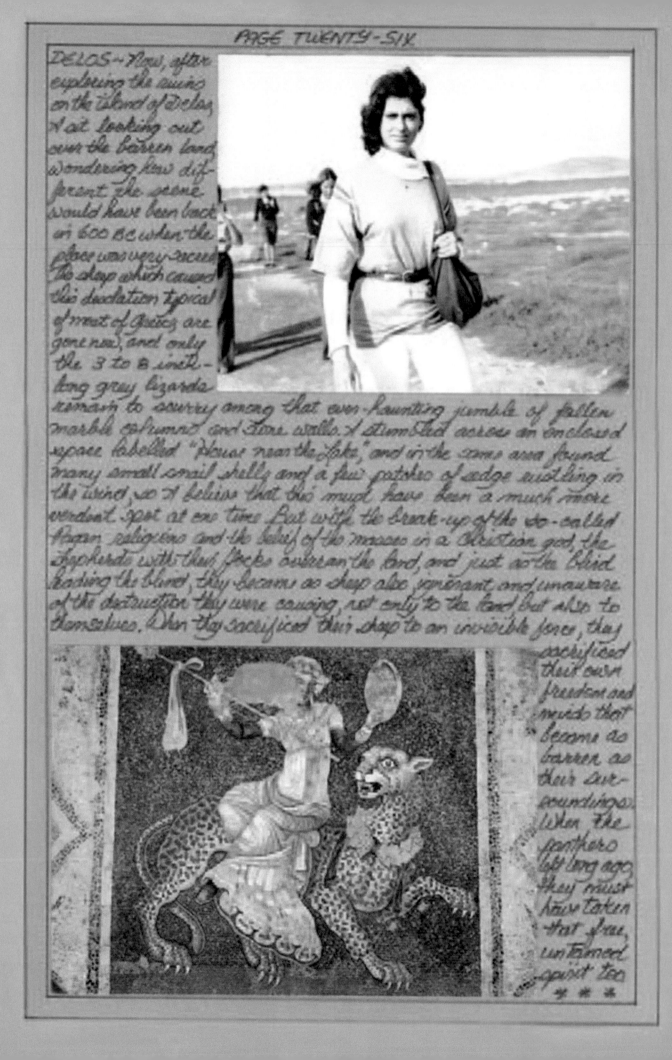

DELOS ~ Now, after exploring the ruins on the island of Delos, I sat looking out over the barren land wondering how different the scene would have been back in 600 BC when the place was very sacred. The sheep which caused this desolation typical of most of Greece are gone now, and only the 3 to 8 inch-long grey lizards remain to scurry among that awe-haunting jumble of fallen marble columns and stone walls. I stumbled across an enclosed space labelled "House near the Lake," and in the same area found many small snail shells and a few patches of sedge rustling in the wind, so I believe that this must have been a much more verdant spot at one time. But with the break-up of the so-called Pagan religions and the belief of the masses in a Christian god, the shepherds with their flocks overran the land, and just as the blind leading the blind, they became as sheep also, ignorant and unaware of the destruction they were causing, not only to the land but also to themselves. When they sacrificed their sheep to an invincible force, they sacrificed their own freedom and minds that became as barren as their surroundings. When the panthers left long ago, they must have taken that free, untamed spirit too.

* * *

DILOS

Five miles across the sea from Mikonos lies the island of Dilos, the religious center of the ancient Aegean world. It was on this majestic island that Leto, the daughter of the Titans Coeus and Phoebe, gave birth to the divine twins Apollo and Artemis, while father Zeus kept watch against his jealous wife Hera, on Mount Kinthos. No births were allowed on the island after that and Dilos was declared sacred to the gods.

The summit of Mount Kinthos has been carved as a platform for the shrines of Zeus and Athena. It is from this 388 foot terrace that you can look north to the island of Tinos, west to Siros, Kithnos and Serifos, east to Mikonos and south to Paros and Naxos.

Dilos was a protectorate of the island of Naxos in the sixth century B.C. Naxos had built the Sanctuary of Apollo with its Terrace of the Lions. Here you will find five lean beasts with tapering waists still crouched on their hind legs guarding the shrine.

The Macedonian kings and Attalus of Pergamos contributed three huge porticoes leading to the vast Hypostyle Hall, that was used as a sort of exchange and general meeting place for traders. There were several markets, a 43 tier theatre, gymnasium, stadium and luxury villas decorated with exquisite mosaics.

ARTEMIS ~ GODDESS OF THE HUNT.

All this sumptuous prosperity ended when in 88 B.C. a hostile fleet massacred 20,000 inhabitants. Twenty years later pirates sacked the port and the emporium became a sanctuary, and, finally, with the decline of religion, a museum. Much of the priceless artistic treasures are scattered throughout the Mediterranean as a result of the plundering. But there is still a lovely statuary to be seen. Precious mosaics, vases and jewelry are now preserved in the museum.

Oct. 29th (Wed.) 30th - four while days have flown by and I look wrote in this book, and these days exist to but a blur in my mind-what hopes and long rides in the ferries now no longer mean experiences for me but quite uncomfortable ones, for I must brave the smoke inside or the cold winds and spray outside, plus nowadays, with the autumn conditions, the boats toss about, and I am forced to listen to many people getting seasick. (They say that simply turning on the water faucet makes a Greek woman a bit queasy so can you imagine...?) I was lucky to be facing the last trip from Thera to Iráklion on the northeast coast of Crete, so I was quite fit on the journey, but otherwise, I would have been just as miserable too. One good result of a ferry ride, the one from Síphnos to Thera, was my meeting with two Canadian girls, Jackie and Helen, both nurses in the same Vancouver hospital, and perhaps because they are a bit less naïve and more down to earth than most American girls, I have continued to travel with them since our first introduction. All three of us shared a room together that first night, and found ourselves to be compatible enough to go on to Crete. I suppose that travelling with another livens things up for them, and as for myself, it is a wonderful learning and sharing experience, but no matter where or with whom I am, I must have some free moments alone in order to think, find refreshment and spiritual survival, for after a time amid the noise, crowds and meaningless conversations, I start to feel my energy draining.

CLIFFS BELOW FIRA, THE MAIN TOWN OF THERA (SANTORINI) AND THE STAIRWAY ✩ FOR THE MULES, THE ONLY MEANS OF ACCESS FROM THE DOCKS TO THE PLATEAU ABOVE.

On Thera, which is a bit unfriendly, as far as the inhabitants of the main town are concerned, I willingly became a part of the youthful crowd at a cheap, local taverna that, because of its newly-purchased juke-box, quickly became the biggest gathering center, so Jackie, Helen and I spent a lot of time there with some new friends and fellow travellers, all youth more of an adventuresome mould than most wealthier tourists.

ΤΛ 229673

ΕΙΣΙΤΗΡΙΟΝ ΔΡΧ DR. 5

We three also joined with a few others and rode by muleback to the site of the new (1967) excavations for a Minoan city thought to be Atlantis, and this was my reason for a special pilgrimage to the island. I was very impressed with the archaeological site because it was all covered like a huge warehouse and the different rooms and buildings of the ancient city were sectioned off. Scattered among the dusty walls and along the winding path, were great blocks of wooden filing cabinets filled with broken pottery—evidence of the extremely difficult job of piecing together a lost culture. In one house, there was a simple grave, covered with wilting flowers and belonging to the 73 year old professor who formerly directed the dig, and died when a wall fell on top of him last summer.

ORTHODOX PRIEST ⇩

Having seen enough of Santorini, I was anxious to see Crete, especially because the winds of the Cyclades in the north just refuse to die down even during the day, so when we three arrived to this great island, we headed straight for the southern coast to a small village which turned out to be nothing but a few houses, a couple with rooms to rent, and one "taverna" for the visitors that pass through looking for good, private beaches. The beach here is excellent—very private with soft white sand, so we managed to go skinny-dipping at a private cove, despite the few vans parked down aways, but the owners proved to be very friendly, interesting and informative, so we joined them a-round the campfire under a starry sky. Now, I'm in Agios Nikolaos to get a cholera shot and meet the 2 girls at the bus tomorrow evening.

Agios Nikolaos

Nov. 2 (Sun) 17th hour ~ Well, instead of my two buddies, a note they had sent, arrived over the bus, and it said that they enjoyed Ierapetra, the largest town in the south, quite cheap and nice, but would be a better place if I could join them, especially for Halloween the next day. So I turned up on the 31st ready to provide a bit of excitement for us by leading a seance, but the four American boys that Jackie and Helen had befriended, weren't interested. Supper stretched out into a 2 to 3 hour affair and as the evening dragged on, the Americans left to pursue the night life, leaving us three girls at the table in the restaurant. But it seems that at this point the tension of their travelling together had come to a high point, and they broke into a heavy discussion, letting all come out into the open. I offered my welcomed opinion until Skip, one of the American boys (who was actually travelling alone but joined the others a week ago) came back and told me enough about his experiences in Egypt to convince me not to chance going to the Arab countries. I had heard similar reports recently, so it didn't take long to decide to go straight to Israel. Later on in the "watching house" we joined other voyagers to share our travel experiences.

KRITI (CRETE)

In about 3,000 B.C. an enterprising chieftain had the brilliant idea to lead his people from Asia Minor to this isle blessed by nature on which Neolithic man had already prospered for some thousand years. This first — a word you will constantly encounter in Cretan history and culture — Minos left his name as title to his successors, who united the various principalities into the first maritime empire in history, to eventually bring most of the Aegean islands and even part of the mainland under its sway.

Europe's first royal dynasty naturally claimed divine ancestry of the very highest. No one less than Zeus would do, to carry the lovely maiden Europe on his broad back to «Kriti», where she gave birth to the first European, the original Minos, who became after his death the first judge in the underworld. Zeus came to her not as mightiest of the Olympian gods, but in the guise of a white bull, an animal strangely attractive to the ladies of Europe's somewhat eccentric family.

The first bullfights were held there, but they were nothing as simple as confrontations with a sword. The participants took the bull by the horns and somersaulted over the huge beasts. The last Minos' wife gave birth to a Minotaur, half man, half bull. To hide this startling offspring, the long-suffering husband built a labyrinth in which the Minotaur was imprisoned, and where he feasted on youths and maidens. When he was slain by Theseus, who escaped with the help of Minos' daughter Ariadne, the first great cycle of legends reached its climax, to provide poets, playwrights and composers with an everlasting source of inspiration. But long before the dramatic end of the Minoan dynasty, the first sophisticated court in Europe had gone through many familiar aspects of fashion : bikinis, topless, flounced skirts, fantastic hairdos for men and women, besides having achieved a standard of plumbing not equalled until our own times. The elegance of court life is superbly illustrated in the frescoes of Knossos palace, whose bathrooms and other sanitary arrangements are no less impressive on the practical side.

In about 1,400 B.C., the downfall of this splendid civilization came about due to several causes: earthquake and invasion, political and artistic decadence. Invasions by a succession of conquerors remarkable even in the disaster - prone Eastern Mediterranean. Finally, Kriti was ready for a completely different kind of invasion.

Tourists, anxious for new horizons, discovered in Kriti the ideal holiday combination of interesting sites and comfortable relaxation. It was the answer to the vacationist's prayer with its delightful climate, geography, history, art and more comforts than home.

* * *

KNOSSOS ~ Nov. 9 (Saturd.) 15th hour ~ This hour finds me well and peaceful, perhaps more so than even yesterday; for, being in Herklio, the capital and urban center of Crete, I have visited the Archaelog. Museum just this morning, and now rest on a flat stone beneath a grand old pine which shelters also the remains of what is labelled "the dean Rest House," part of the Palace of Knossos. I have visited other museums and sites before, but never walked away with such a feeling of being cleansed and purified. In a matter of hours I feel lighter and with a sterner dedication to my purpose in life. Perhaps I have found part of myself in these painted vases, frescoes & incised precious stones. Only a special pilgrimage to this piece of earth could have returned to me a lost part of myself, to shown me a different manifestation of my essence. What really engages me to sit on this stone and write these words, was the pastoral scene in the valley just below: the cart & path harvested and well tried by 2 young women & an older man who now stands near a small cart heaped with huge heads of cabbage; an acre of grape vines turning a dull orange; a half-hidden row of orange trees with almost ripened fruit, & at the edge of the garden hiding 2 palm trees, is the quaint peasant house. But a beautiful black dog intrigues me the most as I idly sit here in thought.

Man added

Palaces ever since about 2,000 B.C. The first regal edifice rose at Knossos, to be destroyed in about 1,700 B.C. by an earthquake that divided the Palace Period into two equal parts preceding the final catastrophe. Schliemann's unerring archaeological instinct, which led him to so many amazing discoveries, first identified the unimpressive mound 5 kilometres from Iraklion, but it took the flair and financial resources of Sir Arthur Evans to bring to light the lost splendour only vaguely remembered from Homeric descriptions. The vast complex of the second Great Palace consisted of large courts, sacred ways and altars: the west wing given over to religious functions which played so important a part in the life of the priest-king; even its great throne room with the oldest throne in the world still in place can be seen and the east section containing the royal apartments with ingenious light wells and comfortable bathrooms. Workshops, the laundry with an up-to-date water and drainage system; the huge northern portal; and the theatre, where the king and court watched bull leaping, their favourite sport, are still there as well.

The downward tapering wooden columns, supporting a many-storeyed timber framework overlaid with gypsum, were hardly suited to withstand destructive earthquakes and fire. Rubble alone supported the delicate fabric remaining, but thanks to a partial re-building in concrete, chosen for technical as well as financial reasons, the legend of the Minotaur's fearful labyrinth becomes understandable along endless corridors, staircases and chambers decorated with superb frescoes in intensive blue, green and the red of congealing blood. Maritime designs are to be seen in the private apartments, and illustrations of court life come alive in the state rooms.

Nov. 13 (Thurs) 11th hour. Just hearing the theme of Zorba the Greek being piped from 2 different record shops on a street in the old city of Rhodes. I think it quite strange, for all during the last month when the tune has played in my mind, not once did I hear it until this last morning in Greece before taking an expensive boat ride to Turkey. Politics had banned the popular melody and political hatred had made connections between these two neighbors more difficult. I have the money to get there but must find work to keep going. I was not able to do portraits here on the most popular tourist island because of the tours, so my new friend, Anna, and I just took it easy, our stay livened by a small earthquake yesterday morning.

RODOS (RHODES)

First colonized by the Minoans and Mycenaeans, Rodos began its rise to prosperity after the arrival of the Dorians in the 11th century B.C. They founded three cities - Ialisos, Kamiros and Lindos - and, by the 18th century B.C., Rodos had become a flourishing crossroads for trade between East and West.

In the 5th century B.C., the three cities of Rodos founded a common centre of administration near the site of the modern capital. In this new city a brilliant culture soon developed and the wealthy Rodians adorned their capitals with magnificent temples, theatres, stadiums and statues.

In the 2nd century B.C., however, the Romans took control of Greece. They competed with Rodos for trade and stripped the island of some 3,000 sculptures which were taken to Rome. The island's prosperity disappeared and it wasn't until the 14th century A.D. that Rodos rose to prominence again.

In 1306, the Genoese, then in possession of Rodos, sold the island to the Knights of St John who had been driven from the Holy Land by the Moslems. The Knights fortified Rodos and established themselves in this stronghold while they continued their mission of defending Jerusalem.

The Knights of St John occupied Rodos for more than 200 years until, in 1522, Suleiman the Magnificent laid siege to the island and the Knights were forced to abandon Rodos to the Turks. The Turkish occupation lasted until 1912 when the Italians captured the island. During the 35 years they controlled Rodos, the Italians devoted themselves to archaeological excavations and restorations and to building a new town adjacent to the medieval city of the Knights of St John. Until, finally, after the Second World War, Rodos was freed and, in 1947, was officially reunited with Greece.

100 LEPTA = 1 DRACHMA

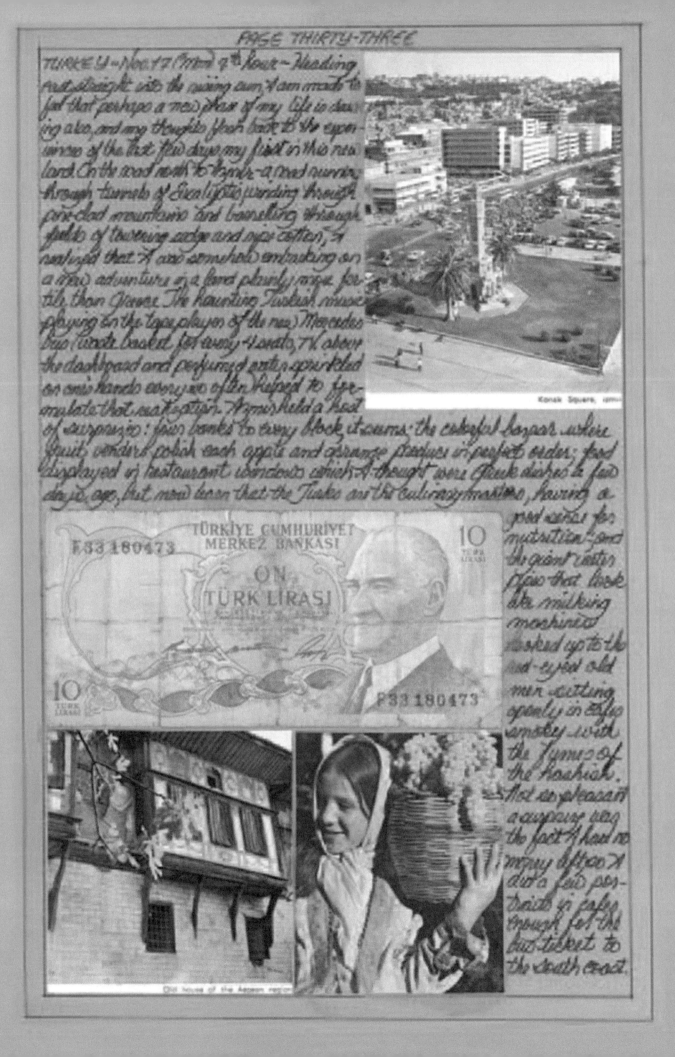

TURKEY — Nov. 17 (Mon) 9th hour — Heading east straight into the rising sun, I am made to feel that perhaps a new phase of my life is dawning also, and my thoughts flash back to the experiences of the last few days, my first in this new land. On the road north to Izmir — a road running through tunnels of Eucalyptii, winding through pine-clad mountains and travelling through fields of towering sedge and ripe cotton, I realized that I was somehow embarking on a new adventure in a land plainly more fertile than Greece. The haunting Turkish music playing on the tape player of the new Mercedes bus (Watts based far away, Sanato, TV above the dashboard and perfumed water sprinkled on our hands every so often helped to formulate that realization. Izmir held a host of surprises: four banks to every block it seems; the colorful bazaar where fruit vendors polish each apple and arrange their produce in perfect order; food displayed in restaurant windows which I thought were Greek dishes days ago, but now learn that the Turks are the culinary masters, having a good sense for nutrition — and the giant water flow that look like milking machines hooked up to the bad-eyed old men sitting openly in the smokey with the fumes of the hashish. Not so pleasant a surprise was the fact I had no money after so I did a few pastries in cafes enough for the bus ticket to the south coast.

Konak Square, Izmir

Old house of the Aegean region

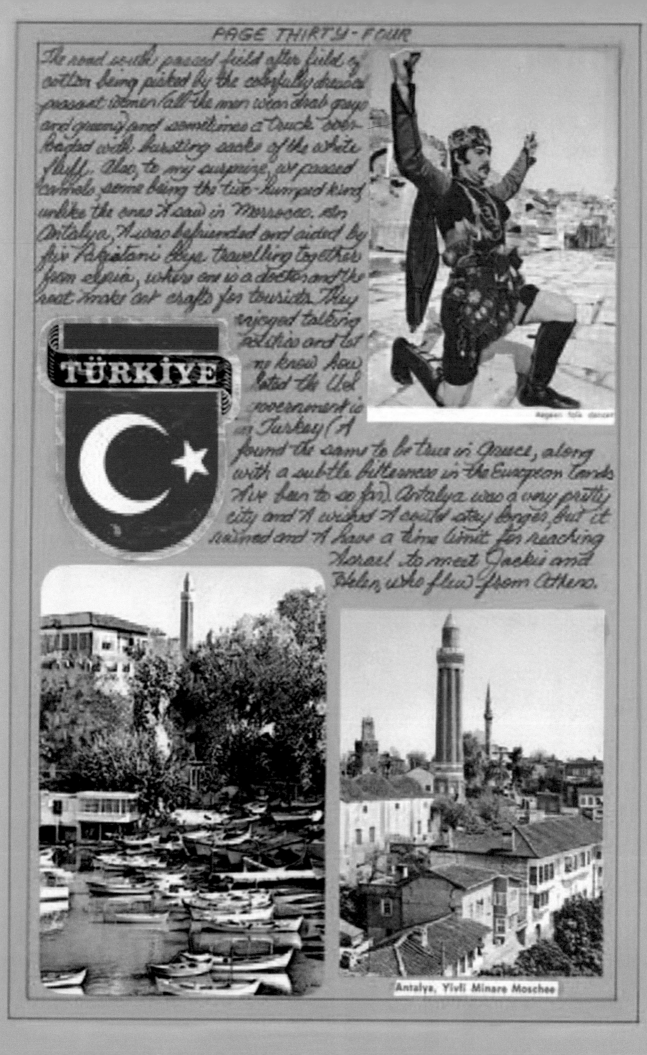

The road which passed field after field of cotton being picked by the colorfully dressed peasant women (all the men wear drab grays and greens) and sometimes a truck overloaded with bursting sacks of the white fluff. Also, to my surprise, we passed camels, some being the two-humped kind, unlike the ones I saw in Morrocco. In Antalya, I was befriended and aided by five Pakistani boys travelling together from Libya, where one is a doctor and the rest make art crafts for tourists. They enjoyed talking politics and let me know how rotten the Wed government is in Turkey (A found the same to be true in Greece, along with a subtle bitterness in the European lands we've been to so far). Antalya was a very pretty city and I wished I could stay longer, but it rained and I have a time limit for reaching Israel to meet Jackie and Helen, who flew from Athens.

Aegean folk dancer

Antalya, Yivli Minare Moschee

Oct 20 (Thurs) 14th hour—I'm looking down on the same snow-capped peaks that I first saw last night, while travelling by bus under a full moon;—an express bus that took 15½ hours from Adana, largest city in the south, to Istambul, to get this thrice-weekly flight for Tel-Aviv. How, you may be asking, did I get myself here. First, Cyprus was out because there are no boats or flights from the Turk side to Israel. While coming out of the ferry boat office in Mersin, where I recieved this information, I bumped into a young man going to Adana, where I hoped to catch a flight to Israel, but after giving me a lift to the airport we learned that only domestic flights go through that city. My new friend, Harlin, realized the near hopelessness of my plight and helped me immensely with all my needs. I recieved an American $10 bill for the money I made at the Istambul Airport while waiting for this flight, and with it I shall enter Israel!

A nomad tent - Mersin

Maiden Castle Beach - Mersin

A General view - Adana

A TYPICAL ISRAELI BEAUTY

72nd hour — Now, as I sit on my bed in a Youth Hostel in Tiberias Jackie and Helen in two other bunks, I can relax and think about my first impressions of Israel, which rushed through my weary head during the bus rides to Tel Aviv from the Ben-Gurion Airport, then to this city on the Sea of Galilee, or Lake of Tiberias. The first thing that really struck me was the lack of a peasant population. Instead, the place is filled by young, sunned, hearty-looking "Kibbutzniks," filling the streets and buses, wearing very simple, functional clothing and carrying only one small bag of their possessions. Since three years of military service are required for both boys and girls at the age of 18, Israel is overrun with soldiers in olive green or khaki, the boys with machine guns and the girls mostly with just a tote bag since they do work other than combat. They all seem to have an air of intelligence and a knowledge of English as I had expected, but I was surprised at their serious nature, I suppose understandable in a nation at war. Jackie and Helen, who have been in Israel for about 2 weeks, have a more experienced opinion. To them, the people are sneaky, selfish, aggressive and impatient. The young men (and the country were overrun with them) spend most of their leisure time hustling women, and because of this, the girls are a bit disappointed with Israel. I can understand this, for one cannot enjoy a different culture if one has to constantly put up with hassles, taunts and interruptions from the childish members of the opposite sex. At any rate, I hope it doesn't interfere with my work in this wealthy new country, but tomorrow I shall know for sure.

PROPAGANDA "KIBBUTZNIK" FED TO TOURISTS

WHAT ZIONISM MEANS

By Misha Louvish

After the vote in which Zionism was condemned by some of the most dictatorial, oppressive and backward countries in the United Nations, it is worth while recalling what the term really means. The simplest way of doing this is to quote the fundamental paragraphs of Israel's Proclamation of Independence, which was promulgated on 14 May 1948, on the eve of the Arab invasion of Palestine in defiance of the world organization's decision on the establishment of a Jewish State:

"In the Land of Israel the Jewish people came into being. In this Land was shaped their spiritual, religious and national character. Here they lived in sovereign independence. Here they created a culture of national and universal import, and gave to the world the eternal Book of Books.

"Exiled by force, still the Jewish people kept faith with their Land in all the countries of their dispersion, steadfast in their prayer and hope to return and here revive their political freedom.

"Fired by this attachment of history and tradition, the Jews in every generation strove to renew their roots in the ancient Homeland, and in re-

cent generations they came home in their multitudes...

"In 1897 the First Zionist Congress met at the call of Theodor Herzl... and gave public voice to the right of the Jewish people to national restoration in their Land.

"This right was acknowledged in the Balfour Declaration on 2 November 1917 and confirmed in the Mandate of the League of Nations, which accorded international validity to the historical connection between the Jewish people and the Land of Israel, and to their right to re-establish their National Home...

"On 29 November 1947 the General Assembly of the United Nations adopted a resolution calling for the establishment of a Jewish State in the Land of Israel, and required the inhabitants themselves to take all measures necessary on their part to carry out the resolution. This recognition by the United Nations of the right of the Jewish people to establish their own State is irrevocable.

"It is the natural right of the Jewish people, like any other people, to control their own destiny in their sovereign State..."

TIBERIAS

TIBERIAS is located on the western shore of the Sea of Galilee (Lake of Tiberias) at 670 feet below sea level. The city was founded in the beginning of the first century C.E. by Herod Antipas, son of Herod the Great, who named it after the Roman Emperor Tiberius. It soon became a spiritual centre of Judaism, attracting many scholars and rabbis. The famous philosopher Maimonides, called Rambam, (Rabbi Moses Ben Maimon) is buried here.

Ever since the Roman period, the city's hot springs have attracted visitors from far away. Today, those in need of treatment avail themselves of a modern bathhouse with the latest equipment and facilities.

The Sea of Galilee and its surroundings are closely connected with the life of Jesus, who spent his manhood here. The Gospels relate how he walked on the waters of the lake and multiplied the loaves and fishes at Tabgha, they describe the Sermon on the Mount (Mount of Beatitudes) and the synagogue of Capernaum where he preached. The River Jordan flows through the lake from North to South.

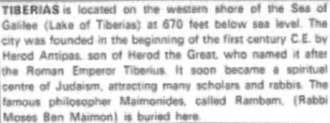

TIBERIAS, 1913

ישראל
ISRAEL

Nov. 30th (Sunday) 8th hour—

It is Sunday, the first day of the Jewish week, for yesterday was Sabbath a whole day of rest, from Friday sundown to Saturday sundown. It is also the last day of this month, and even though I am still in Tiberias, it seems like another town since I moved out of the Youth Hostel yesterday, into this hospice run by a minister of the Church of Scotland. The building, made entirely of stone, used to be a hospital, and the garden, pathways and simply the spontaneity of the structure, give the place a charming and peaceful atmosphere. This morning I had breakfast (included in the $1.50 daily price) in a sunny dining room overlooking the Sea of Galilee, and compared to the dorm-style living of the hostel, which was very expensive, the privacy and homeyness of this place is heavenly. This past week and a half I have been drawing portraits as well as painting designs on two cars (one, a horse's head on the door of a "Mustang", and a dragon on the hood of a red sportscar). Most of my business seems to be with just the young male population because there are few tourists this time of year; the middle-aged and elderly are too old, ugly or religious, and the girls, not half as numerous as the boys are too shy. Consequently, I've had to lower my prices to $2.50 for pencil, $4.00 for charcoal and $5.00 for pastel, so I make on average of $16 for on a normal working day. For odd jobs I charge $1.50 an hour. On my only days off, I have stayed inside to work on this book, and so far haven't taken any side trips, but have only seen the town quite verdant with palms and flowers, and even more curious, it is below sea level. The countryside contains many different "kibbutzim" and once in a while, I'll meet one or two people taking a two-day rest from their labors on one. They tell me that there are many kinds with anywhere from 100 to 1000 people, some being families living in private cabins, volunteers who work full time or those few studying the law or religion, part time. I've heard of one kibbutz where the parents put their children in school, only visiting them for 2 hours a day and perhaps on Sabbath. On another kibbutz the people eat a primitive diet lacking any kind of animal or bread product. They have a reputation of looking very young and healthy even in old age. I tried that diet for a short while but its difficult while living in regular society. One must join a kibbutz for at least 2 months, so I shall not be sharing that experience now, but perhaps on another visit.

*   *   *   *   *

Dec. 3rd (Wed) 9th hour ~ Last night I was invited to a Jewish wedding, Israeli-Style, by a taxi-driver buddy who helps me drum up business. He is the 2nd cousin of the bride. At eight we walked into the dining room of the Quiet Beach Hotel where the wedding guests were sitting at tables listening to lively music played by the young members of a rock band, while they were eating the pickled things and picnic-type salads set on the tables along with beer and soda. The bride 22 years old and one of those dark Israeli girls with a beautifully sculptured face, was dressed in a long, white dress dotted with tiny pink flowers, and sat in the center of the large room on a throne-like platform in front of the bandstand. The groom, handsome but with an aged face, was dressed in a light mocha suit, and just wandered around near his bride and the head table where the close family members sat. The girl's father dressed in white Hebrew robes and sitting next to his third wife (divorced the other two) looked to be about 85 years old and people had to help him get around. When enough guests had arrived, the bride and groom walked to the opposite end of the room while the chair was taken off the platform and a canopy decorated with Jewish symbols was set up in its place. Being the 5th day of Hanukkiah, five candles were lit up on a tall Menorah, and while singing the "Hanukkiah" song, the men and boys put paper napkins from the tables on their heads if they lacked a skull cap. Lead by two candle-wielding children, a girl and boy, the bride with her mother and uncle (father being too old) followed by the groom with his parents, marched slowly but not too solemnly in the noisy and almost disinterested crowded room, to the platform and stood there under the canopy while the Rabbi, son of a very famous Rabbi in the area, blessed the couple by passing some around the tight circle. The groom stomped on the glass, breaking it with hardly a sound, then the Rabbi read the contract saying that if there was a divorce, the husband would give his wife so much money, etc. A white cloth was rested over the couple's heads while the Rabbi chanted special passages from the "Torah," thus ending the formal ceremony. Everyone sat down to prepare for dinner, but only after the waiters trooped around the darkened room carrying sparklers as the guests clapped their hands. The meal was quite simple and modest, not living up to my preconceived ideas of Jewish weddings, and for dessert we had apples, oranges and grapefruit taken from a huge fruitstand, since the 2 families took home the cake. Thus, at 11 PM, after dancing for awhile, ended my first Jewish wedding.

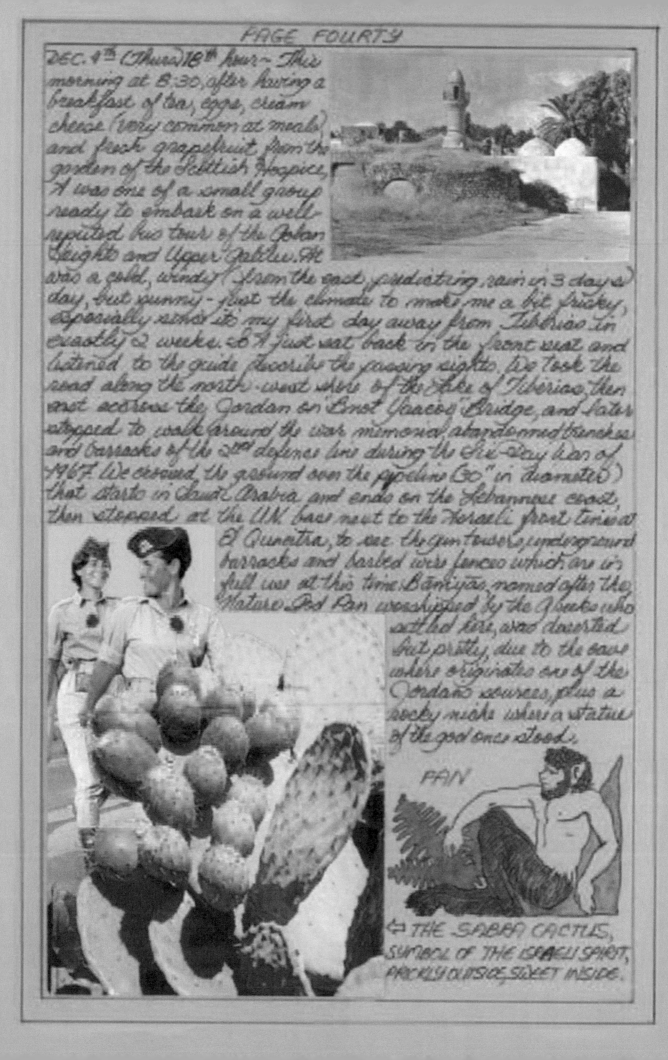

DEC. 4th (Thurs) 18th hour ~ This morning at 8:30, after having a breakfast of tea, eggs, cream cheese (very common at meals) and fresh grapefruit from the garden of the Scottish Hospice, I was one of a small group ready to embark on a well-reputed bus tour of the Golan Heights and Upper Galilee. It was a cold, windy (from the east, predicting rain in 3 days) day, but sunny – just the climate to make me a bit fricky, especially since it's my first day away from Tiberias in exactly 2 weeks. So I just sat back in the front seat and listened to the guide describe the passing sights. We took the road along the north-west shore of the Lake of Tiberias, then east across the Jordan on "Bnot Yaacov" Bridge, and later stopped to walk around the war memorial, abandoned trenches and barracks of the 3rd defense line during the Six-Day War of 1967. We crossed the ground over the pipeline (30" in diameter) that starts in Saudi Arabia and ends on the Lebanese coast, then stopped at the U.N. base next to the Israeli front lines at El Quneitra, to see the gun towers, underground barracks and barbed wire fences which are in full use at this time. Baniyas, named after the Nature God Pan worshipped by the Greeks who settled here, was deserted but pretty, due to the cave where originates one of the Jordan sources, plus a rocky niche where a statue of the god once stood.

PAN

⟶ THE SABRA CACTUS, SYMBOL OF THE ISRAELI SPIRIT, PRICKLY OUTSIDE, SWEET INSIDE.

The mysterious Druse people live in separate hill villages, the largest called the "Gun Tower", and some of the Druce are fair-complexioned due to intermixing with Crusaders who built a string of fortresses from nearby hilltops to the Mediterranean during the 13th century. Their secret religion is known only by certain men who wear a different headpiece to distinguish them from the rest, and it dictates that women be totally equal with men, so that a couple marries for life and even if the wife dies first, her husband cannot remarry. The nature reserve of Dan, with its clear, rushing springs and lush vegetation forming "tunnels" around the twisting paths, was a paradise to where I would love to return. It broke

TEL DAN (TEL EL KADI)
PLACE OF THE ANCIENT CITY OF DAN

off from the group and went exploring for about 10 minutes, not nearly long enough, for each time a tempting side path cropped up, I had to reject it and think about heading back. Nearby we crossed the River Dan (judge) and another stream, the two other sources of the Jordan and as the legend goes, God had to be called down to settle the quarrel between the three as to which one would be the most important so God told them to join together and make the Jordan. Another beautiful site was the flower garden in bloom at the guest house of the kibbutz near the museum and archeological site of Hebron, the great Canaanite city of 40,000, which was destroyed by Joshua 3,200 years ago. We passed through the new large settlement of Qiryat Shamona, an example of a city where foreign immigrants are sent after a six month orientation period when they learn Hebrew and tour Israel. They are given accommodations and helped with their profession, but many sent to this city leave after feeling threatened by the shells dropped from nearby Lebanon every 4 or 5 months. The kibbutz, 100 meters from the border is spared because, as the Jews claim, the Arabs know any such scale would only strengthen these hearty, determined pioneers.

*　　*　　*　　*　　*　　*

Dec. 13th (Sat) 11th hour ~ During the past week in Tiberias, I had not been so preoccupied with work, for I have found the young Jews to be lacking in a serious approach to their business dealings with me, and once they realized I would have nothing to do with them socially (they are selfish, crude and childish) word got around this tightly-knit town to ignore me. Indeed, my experience here centered around a man I met the night before I went on the Golan Heights tour. On that night, one of the first things Jacob told me was that he is a Christian born in Jerusalem. Now, that means he an Arab of former Palestine, one of the majority who stayed during the last three decades. His father who died four years ago, was the leader of the Greek Orthodox community in Jerusalem; a well-known and respected man remembered even today, and during the war he fought to keep their old house just 100 meters from the Church of the Holy Sepulcher, the site of Christ's tomb. Ah, you must have been wondering when or if I would reveal any of my so-called romantic ventures, but probably thought up to now that they were too private. Well, to be honest with you, from the start of this book in September, I have not met anyone who filled all my thoughts or for one second broke my will to surge onward in my travels. With many I have freely given my time, advice, energy and courage, but rarely anything more. Since leaving Kony 10 months ago, I have faced many situations which provided challenges to my strength, flexibility and good judgement, so therefore I am not the same person who with a lot more uncertainty than was chosen at the time left last written to embark on a new journey. Pride in my achievements has grown, along with my self-respect, and I have managed to preserve my honesty without being too open. So what about Jacob? Being 32 years old and a person with much intelligence, integrity, independence, qualities I treasure in myself, he immediately emanated a power and complexity. Once a kindred spirit was mutually recognized, we realized on that first night during a lengthy discussion, that our relationship would grow into a strong, spiritual one, with an understanding of each other's life goals, and that I would leave as planned, taking with me and leaving behind all the benefits and results of the exchanges we made during my stay. Yesterday, as we drove into Jerusalem, the sky above forming a halo of pink, orange and yellow as we entered the "golden city" during the sunset's most gorgeous moments, breathing the cold, still mountain air. *

JACOB

Jerusalem

Jerusalem, capital city of Israel, is the highlight of any visit to this country. For the thousands of visitors who tread its streets each year, Jerusalem has a power and a dignity all its own. Since the days when King David made the city his royal capital some three thousand years ago, Jerusalem has held a central place in the stirring history of this land. It was here, high on the Judean Hills, that King Solomon built his Temple. Babylonians, Persians, Greeks, Romans, Muslims, Crusaders and Turks, each in turn fought for and conquered the enduring city. Today, after a period of twenty five years, Jerusalem has been reunited and persons of all faiths once again have free access to the Holy shrines in and around the Old City.

Modern Jerusalem is the proud home of Israel's state institutions, its Knesset (parliament), government buildings, Supreme Court, Chief Rabbinate, the Hebrew University, the Israel Museum and many other national and cultural foundations.

Many of the 300,000 persons comprising the re-united city's population are new immigrants who have arrived in Israel since the establishment of the State in 1948, making their own invaluable contribution to Jerusalem's varied and colourful aspects, living busy lives in its modern suburbs, and breathing new life into this ancient city.

Ancient and modern exist side-by-side in Jerusalem. Archaeological treasures are found in the midst of newly landscaped parks and gardens. Traditional forms of worship are observed both by venerable patriarchs and young University students. And present-day architecture blends 20th century lines with the mellow stone quarried from the surrounding Judean Hills.

The sanctity of the city is best felt on Saturday — the Jewish Sabbath, when Jerusalem's streets are filled with strolling family groups, made vivid by the varied festive garb proudly worn by its many communities. Public transport ceases on Friday before sunset and all is peace and calm — the very embodiment of the spirit enshrined in the name Jerusalem.

On Fridays and Sundays most Moslem and Christian places of business are closed.

JERUSALEM WITHIN THE WALLS

1. Church of St. Anne	10. Cust. Terra Santa
2. Ch. of Flagellation	11. Christ Church
3. Ecce Homo Arch	12. Armenian Church
4. Ethiopian Monast.	13. Dormition Church
5. The Holy Sepulchre	14. David's Tomb
6. Ch. of Redeemer	15. Hurva Synagogue
7. Ch. of St. John	16. Robinson's Arch
8. Latin Patriarchate	17. El Aqsa Mosque
9. Greek Patriarchate	18. Solomon's Stables

The Stations on the Way of the Cross from Pilate's Judgement place in Antonia to the Holy Sepulchre.

I Jesus is condemned to death	VIII Jesus meets the city's women
II Jesus receives his cross	IX Jesus falls the third time
III Jesus falls the first time	X Jesus' garments are stripped
IV Mary meets Jesus	XI Jesus is nailed to the cross
V Simon is made to bear the cross	XII Jesus dies on the cross
VI Veronica wipes Jesus' face	XIII Jesus is taken from the cross
VII Jesus falls the second time	XIV Jesus is laid in the sepulchre

"You see the Western Wall, one of the walls which formed the holy of holies of the ancient temple; it is called Gate of Mercy, and all Jews resort thither to say their prayers near the wall of the courtyard".

(The Diary of Benjamin of Tudela, 12th century)

"The buildings of Jerusalem are very fine and the stones are larger than in the buildings of the other places that I have seen. The Moslems and also the Jews of this place eat out of one vessel with their fingers, without a napkin, just as the Cairenes do, but their clothes are clean".

(Rabbi Meshullam Ben Menachem of Volterra: Florentine manuscript, 1481)

"Life in Jerusalem is pleasant, its streets are clean, and its inhabitants are men of good will from all walks of life. Hardly a day passes without some stranger coming to visit the city.

People find themselves drawn here — people from all over the world — drawn here as if by some irresistible intangible force".

(Shams ed-Din Abdallah Mohammed ibn Ahmed al-Mukaddasi, Moslem traveller and student of geography and economy, writing of his native Jerusalem, 10th century)

"Perched on its eternal hills, white and domed and solid, massed together and hooped with high grey walls, the venerable city gleamed in the sun. So small! Why, it was no larger than an American village of four thousand inhabitants. Jerusalem numbers only fourteen thousand people. A fast walker could go outside the walls of Jerusalem and walk entirely around the city in an hour. I do not know how else to make one understand how small it is".

(Mark Twain: Innocents Abroad, 1867)

Gates of the Old City: Eight in number, the gates of the Old City each have a multitude of legends and history which have grown up around them.

Zion Gate can be entered from Mt. Zion; it is known to the Arabs as David's Gate, since it was from here that pilgrims went to visit King David's grave. **Jaffa Gate** marks the start of the road leading from Jerusalem to the coast — hence its name (after the leading port of this country in ancient times). Today, the road leads to the left of the gate, which is most easily approached from the Citadel. **The New Gate**, which is in the Christian section of the Old City, was first opened in 1889, to facilitate the connection with the Christian quarter — a privilege granted the various religious emissaries by permission of the Turkish Sultan. **Damascus Gate**, which leads straight into the oriental market, lies on the northern side of the old walls. In Hebrew it is known as the gate to Shechem, or Nablus, for it marks the start of the road to that city (the road continues to Damascus, hence the English name). Above the gate is an Arabic inscription recording that Sultan Suleiman the Magnificent commanded that the wall and its gates be built. (Bus 3, 12, 27)

Herod's Gate, a short distance away from Damascus Gate, is named for King Herod who did much to beautify the ancient city of Jerusalem. On the Eastern wall of the city, facing the Mount of Olives, is **St. Stephen's Gate** (Known in Hebrew as Sha'ar Ha'arayot — Lions Gate — on account of the lions carved on either side). Legend says that Sultan Suleiman dreamed he would be killed by lions if he did not build a wall around the Holy City. He accordingly built this wall and the lions were carved as a propitiatory gesture. An inscription recording the building of the wall and the Gate is to be found above the Gate, on the inside. Christian tradition says that it was from this site that St. Stephen, the first martyr, was led to his execution. Moslem tradition calls the gate after Mary, the mother of Jesus, who, according to tradition, was born in a house over which was built the nearby St. Anne's church. **The Golden Gate**, which overlooks the Valley of Kidron, is known in Jewish tradition as the Gate of Mercy, since it was here — in former times — that Jews, circling the walls of the city, would pray to God for mercy. Many traditions relate the Golden Gate, which has been walled up for several centuries, to the part it will play in the "end of days". Christian tradition says it was through this gate that Jesus and his disciples walked in procession bearing palm branches. **Dung Gate**, which faces

⇧ INSIDE DAMASCUS GATE

south away from the city, is the lowest of all the gates. Mentioned first in a description of the prophet Nehemiah's tour of the city, it is so called because it marks the place where refuse was thrown beyond the city walls. * * *

(MIDDLE) ST. STEPHENS GATE
(LOWER) THE GOLDEN GATE

Saturday in Jerusalem

Shabbat in Jerusalem is considered to be one of the holier ways to spend the day of rest, and, indeed, so it is in most of Jerusalem, especially in the religious quarters of Meah Shearim and Bayit Vegan.

However, not too far away within the walls of the Old City, a very different scene is in evidence. In the narrow, winding alley-ways leading off the main entrances, the Jaffa Gate and the Damascus Gate, tourists and Israelis from all over the country (Jerusalemites usually avoid the Saturday rush) descend on the ancient marketplace.

For those visiting the Old City for the first time both the goods for sale and the sales pitch will be a novel experience: vases and bowls of colourful glass hailing from Hebronite factories; gaily coloured straw baskets, hand-made carpets from Persia, brass and copperware, little wooden tables made by the Druze and woven camel carpets.

Store owners stand in the doorway beckoning to passers-by with cries of "Welcome, welcome..." "have a look "special price for you". Both buyer and seller seem to enjoy haggling over prices and engaging in superlatives of flattery before settling on a price.

Tucked away in the mosaic of communities that make up Jerusalem's population is the orthodox religious stronghold of Mea Shearim.

Everyday dress consists of black coats reaching below the knees, wide-brimmed black hats, and trousers tucked into knee-high socks. Women cover their heads and reflect their interpretation of modest dress in the form of long-sleeved dresses with hemlines reaching down to their calves.

Its streets, whether narrow and quaint or broad and flat, are lined with double-storey buildings from which delicately framed balconies jut out. Behind these facades are gracious patios, synagogues humming with the reverent incantations of the pious, and yeshivot catering to hundreds of youngsters wearing the traditional side-curls (peyot).

The Sabbath is observed with scrupulous devotion in this sector of Jerusalem and there is much coming and going between Mea Shearim and the Western (Wailing) Wall. On this day visitors will see many of the men wearing the fur hat known as a shstralmel.

Kosher food laws, based on prohibitions from biblical days and widely expanded by commentaries beginning in the days of Ezra the Scribe, are widely observed in the Israeli home and partially followed by Moslems and Druze.

Many restaurants in Israel also follow the religious forms closely, belying with their quality the continental dictum that kosher strictures and haute cuisine are incompatible. Problems arise mainly from the prohibition against eating milk and meat products together. Jewish cooks, with the aid of modern science, have discovered suitable substitutes.

Even outsiders usually know that Jews are forbidden to eat the flesh of the pig. This is because the swine, along with many other animals, fails to fulfil the two requirements for edible animals — that it has a split hoof and that it also chews its cud.

The pig has the split hoof, but is ruled out by the cud law.

Other animals, such as the camel, chew a cud but do not have a split hoof and are, therefore, as strongly forbidden as the pig though perhaps less notorious because less tempting.

In the realm of fish, all seafood on the Jewish menu must have scales and fins. This was once problematic in the days of the mercury-free swordfish, which has scales when young but later sheds them. Naturally, such seafood as lobsters, clams, and oysters which have neither, are forbidden, but also on the blacklist are whales, sharks and porpoises.

Jewish Quarter: Prior to 1948 and the War of Independence, the Jewish quarter of the Old City was located in the south-eastern section, alongside the Western Wall (the Wailing Wall) of the Temple. After the hostilities, Jews were denied access to the Old City and the hundreds of religious and cultural institutions founded and maintained by them throughout the ages were systematically destroyed.

Following the reunification of the city, in June 1967, strenuous efforts are being made to re-establish the many synagogues, talmudical colleges and other centres, as far as possible on the area they previously occupied.

Western Wall: The sole remnant of the Temple, the wall, popularly known as the Wailing Wall, formed the western wall of the Temple courtyard. For many centuries, this has remained Jewry's most sacred shrine, and throughout the exile thousands upon thousands of Jews have made the perilous pilgrimage to the Holy Land to pray before its immense stones. During many periods of history, Jewish prayer in this area was either forbidden or undertaken at risk of life, yet nothing has ever shaken the Jewish people's devotion to this spot. Tradition explains the survival of this one wall as Divine recompense for the labour with which it was built by the poor — for in the building of the Temple it was to the poor people that this humble wall was assigned, and since they could not pay for hired labour, they built it with their own hands. Scores of traditions have grown up around the Wall — one of the most popularly observed is that of writing private petitions and prayers on small slips of paper which are then hidden between the stones — for the eyes of God alone. Another is that of hammering a nail into the Wall before any departure from the Holy Land, in token of assurance that the traveller retains his stake in the land. Although pilgrimage to the Wall takes place every day, special importance is attached to a pilgrimage on the ninth of the month of Av — the anniversary of the destruction of both the Temples at the hands of foreign conquerors.

BLOWING THE "SHOFAR"

⇧ WAILING WALL

READING THE "THORA" ⇨ (BOOK OF THE LAW)

A Walk to the Western Wall

The quickest way by foot to the Western (Wailing) Wall takes you from the Damascus Gate, through the fabled Arab bazaars and past some of the finest examples of Mameluke architecture still standing in the Holy Land.

The Mamelukes were slaves who overthrew their Egyptian masters in the 13th century and went on to rule Palestine until the Ottoman Turks conquered the country in 1517.

As you go through the Damascus Gate observe the Arabs smoking the hookah pipe as they sit on stools outside the restaurants.

The contraption comprises a slender glass jar, a quarter of which is filled with water. A piece of hot coal is placed over dampened tobacco on the opened top. When inhaled through a pipe leading to the water, the smokers swear that it creates visions of a thousand-and-one nights. The hookah pipe is also said to take away the nicotine.

About 100 metres from the Damascus Gate continue along El-Wad Road. Pass by the stalls showing metalware, leatherware, baskets, olive-wood carvings and other handicrafts.

The stalls peter out along the brief stretch of the winding Via Dolorosa when you pass Stations III, IV and V of the last route walked by Jesus.

Turn right into Takiyeh Street and walk up until you come to a building on the left distinguished by black basalt, pink marble and white limestone stripes. This was a theological seminary (Madrasah) when built in 1540 and contains features of both Mameluke and Ottoman architecture. It is still a school.

Climb the steps by the Takiyeh Convent, a little way up on the left. Once a palace, it is now a Moslem orphanage. It was built in 1398 and the Princess es-Sitt Tunshuq, who commissioned it, is buried in the handsome building opposite.

The next building up on the left houses a large carpentry shop. Some authorities believe it was a Moslem soup kitchen established by the wife of Suleiman the Magnificent in the early 16th century.

Return to El-Wad Road and cross over into Ala 'Uddin (Alladin) Street.

On your left and right is the African Quarter of the old city. Nobody knows how or when their forefathers arrived in Jerusalem but they have been here for several centuries.

Their quarter is dank and squalid. On the left they are housed in the 13th century Madrasah Hasaniya which the Ottomans later converted into prison cells for condemned men. It has the oldest Mameluke doorway in Jerusalem.

On the right the Africans are quartered in the 13th century hospice.

Return to El-Wad Road, walk up and turn right into Bab el-Silsileh Road (Street of the Chain). Just before you turn left into Western Wall Road, with the Wailing Wall a few hundred metres away, peek through the iron bars of the windows on your left. The three tombs inside belong to the 13th century Emir Turbat Barakat Khan and his sons.

VIA DOLOROSA ⇧

Temple Mount: The site of the Temple is now occupied by the two largest mosques — el Omar and el Aksa. The Temple, first built by Solomon, later rebuilt by the Jews who returned from Babylonian captivity, and further beautified by Herod, stood atop Mount Moriah, the site on which Abraham prepared to sacrifice Isaac.

Mosque of el-Aksa: Largest of the city's mosques, the el-Aksa (the name designates the furthest point on Mohammed's journey from Mecca to Jerusalem) was originally built by the Ommayad ruler Abdul-Malik, alongside the Mosque of Omar. It was subsequently rebuilt by the Fatimid Khalif Ad-Dahir. The Crusaders turned the building into a church, but when Saladin conquered Jerusalem from them, he speedily restored its status. An earlier mosque is situated under the el-Aksa.

Mosque of Omar: The third most important shrine in Islam (after Mecca and Medina), the Mosque of Omar is built on Mount Moriah, the site of the Temple. An octagonal building of great beauty, it was originally built in 691 by the Ommayad Khalif Abdul Malik Bin Marwan, though later generations have further added to and decorated the rich domed structure. Inside the mosque is a large rock (the mosque is also known as The Dome of the Rock) believed to have marked both the spot on which Abraham prepared to sacrifice Isaac, and the place from which Mohammed rode to heaven astride his famous steed el Burak (Jewish tradition sees the stone as the foundation stone of the Temple). The rock is surrounded by a Crusader grill. Below, down a short flight of stairs, is the Cave of the Prophets.

⇧ SERVING COFFEE IN A BEDUIN TENT.

JERUSALEM, DOME OF THE ROCK

Arab Delights

One experience not to be missed while in Israel is the gastronomic delight of eating in an Arab restaurant.

When you order your first course you'll be surprised at the variety of salads the waiter brings out. In some restaurants the number reaches ten. Most common is humus, a paste made from chickpeas. It has a mild taste and is usually eaten by dipping the pitah in it and then into the plate of Turkish salad made of tomatoes, onions, peppers, garlic and cayenne pepper, which ranges from mild and sweet to very hot. The other salads include tehina, made from sesame paste, served both alone and mixed with chopped parsley, eggplant salad, yoghurt salad, chopped tomatoes and cucumbers in tehina etc., etc.

Succulent veal and lamb served sizzling hot from the oven are Arab specialities, accompanied by saffron rice or chips and salad. If you're lucky they'll have stuffed young pigeon available the day that you visit.

The meal is followed by sweets, made with nuts and honey, the most popular being baclawa and burmeh, and Turkish coffee with hel, cardamom seed. Sip this slowly and savour the strong flavour.

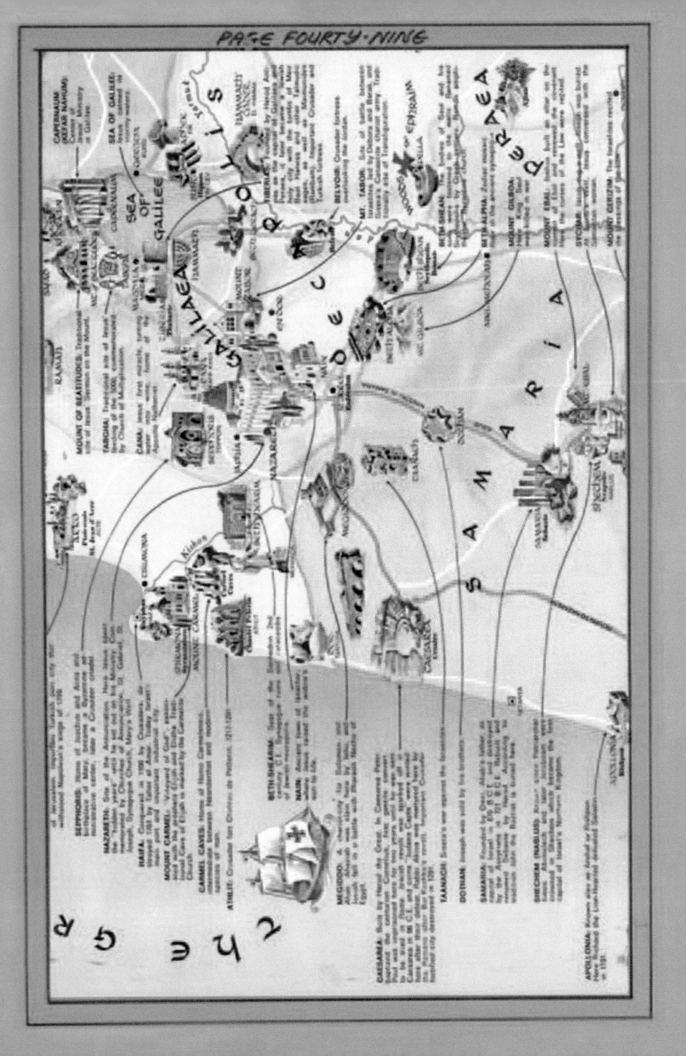

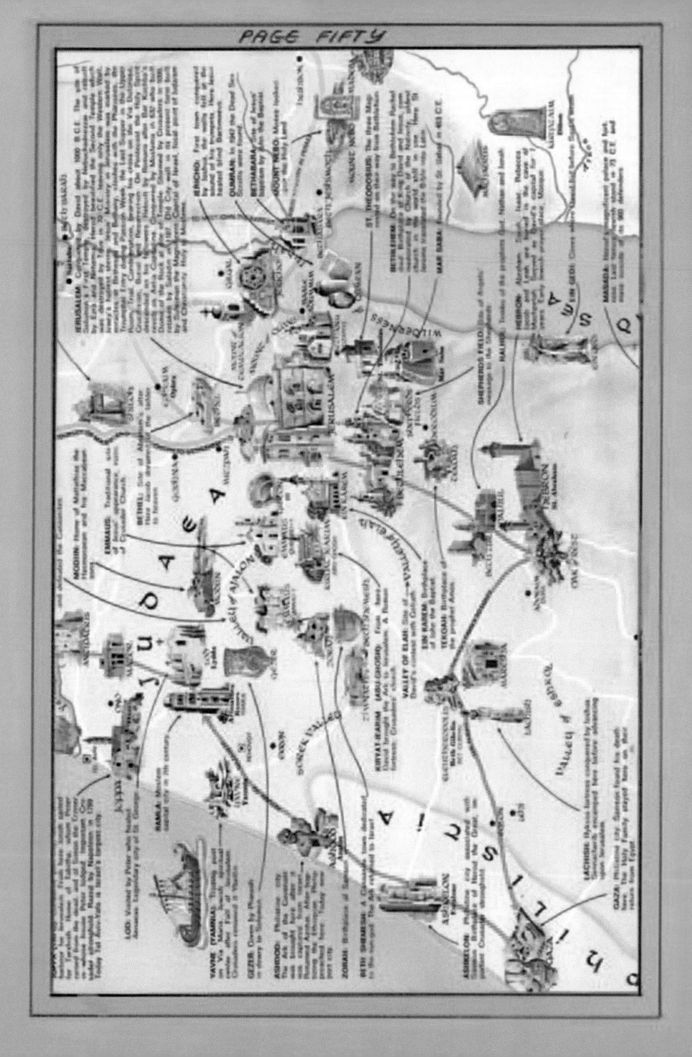

NAZARETH —
THE GROTTO OF THE ANNUNCIATION
In the Basilica of the Annunciation

The Grotto of the Annunciation — a holy chamber that witnessed the salutation of the angel Gabriel. Here the archangel descended from the throne on high to deliver a greeting from the eternal God to Mary, the virgin full of grace. A sacred hour for heaven and earth, the hour of calling and election. Mary is chosen to be the mother of the Son of God. "The Holy Spirit will come upon you, and the power of the Most High will overshadow you; therefore the child to be born will be called holy, the Son of God" (Luke 1: 35).

Thus Mary was privileged to bring Jesus, the Son of God, to the world. "Blessed are you among women, and blessed is the fruit of your womb!" (Luke 1: 42). We can only join Elizabeth in this exclamation of praise, and pray to the Lord, "Let my life too be an unconditional surrender to Your will, Your leadings." Truly, then we shall experience what Jesus said, "Whoever does the will of my Father in heaven is my brother, and sister, and mother" (Matthew 12: 50).

And Mary said, "Behold I am the handmaid of the Lord; let it be to me according to your word." Luke 1: 38

Upon hearing God's holy word,
The Virgin Mary responded
And humbly submitted to His high decree.
Because her love for God was pure,
She gave her will completely,
Consenting to His holy claim on her.

(text of a plaque on the Basilica of the Annunciation in front of the former entrance to the grotto — revised translation)

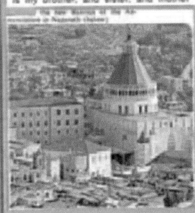

BETHLEHEM — THE NATIVITY GROTTO

A grotto, a small, dark room with crowds of people surging through it. And here, according to the earliest traditions, Jesus was born as a human Child — Jesus, the one Lord, who alone has power to deliver souls from sin and guilt, from fear, distress and despair. Love constrained Jesus, the eternal Son of God, to come to us on earth, to draw very near to us in order to help us. Here He lay as an infant in the manger.

The Word became flesh and dwelt among us.

John 1: 14

Holy Child,
Your light shines brighter
Than sins night and
misery. Triumphantly
You lead the world
from chains of death,
to victory.

When dark is the world today, this Child brings the world the light.

(text of a plaque in the cloister of the Franciscan monastery between the Church of the Nativity and St. Catharine's)

LATIN CONVENT IN BETHLEHEM

BETHLEHEM

A few miles south of Jerusalem, nestling in the Judean hills, lies the little town of Bethlehem. The name of the town means 'House of Bread' suggestive of the fertile valleys and rich olive groves that surround the town. To the east lies the Wilderness of Judah falling down to the Dead Sea.

Bethlehem was already a well-known city in Biblical times. It was here that Rachel the Matriarch died: "And Rachel died and was buried in the way to Ephrath which is Bethlehem. And Jacob set a pillar upon her grave, that is the pillar of Rachel's grave unto this day." (Gen. 35, 19). Lying at the entrance to Bethlehem, Rachel's Tomb is one of the most sacred of Jewish shrines. It was here also that the romance between Boaz and Ruth the Moabite was enacted and where their descendant David the shepherd tended his flocks until called upon by the Prophet Samuel to be King of all Israel.

For Christians, Bethlehem's religious significance derives from the fact that it was here that Jesus was born. Ever since, Bethlehem has been a place of great sanctity and among the most important of all Christian shrines, drawing a multitude of pious pilgrims, especially at Christmas and Easter. The town, whose population is mainly Christian, contains many churches and monasteries. The pealing of church bells and the chanting of monks and priests impart to the town an atmosphere of profound spirituality.

The town's most prominent landmark is the Basilica of the Nativity built on the site of Jesus' birth. Constructed by the Emperor Justinian in 325, it is one of the oldest churches in all Christendom. The Basilica is built like a citadel with defence apparently a major consideration. This is not surprising considering the often violent history of the Holy Land. Each Christmas the Basilica is the site of a vast religious service in which Christians of all denominations participate. There are many other sites of religious interest in Bethlehem. The Milk Grotto, according to tradition, is where the Holy Family took refuge prior to their flight to Egypt and where the Virgin Mary nursed the infant Jesus. The Shepherds' Field is the place where tradition has it shepherds watched over their flocks at the time of Jesus' birth: "And there were in the same country shepherds abiding in the field, keeping watch over their flocks by night. And lo the Lord came upon them and the glory of the Lord shone around about them." (Luke 1, 8).

The town has had a chequered history. In the past 2,000 years it has changed hands many times and been ruled by Romans, Byzantines, Arabs, Crusaders, Mamelukes and Turks. Despite the many centuries of frequently hostile non-Christian rule, which often made pilgrimages difficult and even hazardous, Christians have steadfastly clung to Bethlehem throughout the ages— to this day the population consists mainly of Christians—a measure of the great faith inspired by this little town—the birthplace of Jesus.

THE CHURCH OF THE NATIVITY

CHRISTMAS EVE PROCESSION OF THE LATIN PATRIARCH WITH MANGER SQUARE IN THE BACKGROUND.

Christmas Day - Dec. 25th (Thurs) 17th hour - There are no words to describe the extreme beauty of the sunset in this hour - the "Stratus" clouds spreading across the whole sky like a quilt covering the earth; each puff of bluish-grey lit up A bright orange-pink on one side and those closest to the firey ball are so fluorescent that nothing man-made could ever come close to producing such a wonder. Today I'm a bit sentimental aren't I? Well, its Christmas, and I have had one that I shall never forget, partly, of course, because I'm in Jerusalem with Claude's family, who have treated me with great warmth and affection since my arrival, but also because I spent yesterday in Bethlehem, one of hundreds gathered in "Manger Square" outside the "Church of the Nativity;" hundreds of different people from all parts of the world, all walks of life, and I realized that Christmas in Bethlehem would be the only event that could bring people together like that just for one day. Pilgrims march to Lourdes, but they come in a constant stream day after day; Nations gather at world expositions lasting month's, same with the Olympics etc, but a tiny stone "grotto" in a small city nestled in the hills of "Palestine," can draw these human beings for just one night to pray, to fulfill a lifelong dream like Grandma would have done; but also to appease their curiosity, because, I suppose its the most inspirational place for a Christian to be on Christmas Eve. All the different sects cannot claim Bethlehem for their own on this night however, for that would cause confusion and a conflict in actual observations, so consequently, last night was for the worship by the Latin and Protestant churches.

Christmas in Bethlehem

The celebration of Christmas will commence at 12.30 p.m. on Wednesday, December 24th, when His Beatitude, the Latin Patriarch, heads a procession of clergymen from Jaffa Gate in Jerusalem to Manger Square in Bethlehem, arriving at 1.30 p.m.

At 4.30 p.m. a Protestant service will be held at Shepherds' Field in Bethlehem. From 8.30 to 11.45 p.m. there will be choir performances of Christmas Carols at Manger Square, and at Midnight a Latin Pontifical High Mass will be conducted in the Basilica of the Nativity. The Mass will be relayed over closed circuit television to a huge screen in Manger Square.

Invitations for tourists to the City of Bethlehem may be obtained upon presentation of passports at the Tourist Information Offices in Jerusalem, Tel Aviv, Beer Sheva, Haifa and Netanya (see page 70 for addresses). It should be noted that these invitations do not include entrance to the Basilica of the Nativity for Midnight Mass. There tickets must be obtained from the competent authorities of the Catholic, Latin and Protestant Churches. Those wishing to attend should apply immediately to the Franciscan Custodian of the Holyland, P.O.B. 186, Jerusalem, or ask at the Christian Information Centre, opposite the Citadel, near Jaffa Gate.

Visitors to Bethlehem should be aware that they will be able to travel to the city on the 24th by bus only. No private cars will be allowed. A special post office will operate near Manger Square and all mail will be franked with a special Christmas Day postmark. Shops and restaurants will be open, a special telephone booth for overseas calls will be available, banking services will be available until midnight, and of course, the Tourist Information Office will be operating in Manger Square. Tourists must carry their passports with them at all times.

Special transportation to Bethlehem has been organized by the various bus companies, and information may be had from them or the Government Tourist Information Offices. A regular Jerusalem to Bethlehem bus will leave the Central Bus Station every 30 minutes until 8 p.m.

Please note that the Greek Orthodox Church celebrates Christmas on January 6th, and the Armenian Orthodox Church on January 18th.

We welcome all visitors to the Holyland during this holiday season, and hope that they will enjoy their stay.

Peace on earth and good will to all people!

At 1:30 PM, amid a crowd of young scouts and marching high school bands (their beat conflicting with the Christmas carols piped in the background) and policemen riding spirited Arab mounts, a lines of young, Catholic boys and men dressed in long black robes and frilly white smocks, prepared to receive the Latin Patriarch, who was to become the center of attention for the whole day. He slowly walked towards the church, along with a circle of guards and high church officials from Rome, and with each measured step, he mumbled blessings and reverent words, all in the appearance of deep respect seriousness, and awareness of his divine responsibility. But my mind, as I watched him move, decked in bright pinkish-purple robes, ermine capes and priceless jewels, was not filled with awe or appreciation - in fact what struck me first, cannot be mentioned here out of consideration for the beliefs of some who may read this. Well, I suppose that with the progress and evolution of civilization and technology, caused by man's inevitable desire to make life more complex, we forget the simple little wonders of nature and the human personality, and create new plastic worlds, for the purpose of entertaining our bored minds. To be truthful, as I walked among the crowds of tourists and pesty young Arabs, read the signs like "Nativity Restaurant and Bar," along with shop signs advertising souvenirs and diamonds (an area specialty) and listened to choirs from all over the world singing as the huge Christmas tree glittered in one corner of the square, I was not so inspired, not even entertained, as Grandma would have been with the chance.

HIS HOLINESS, POPE PAUL VI IN THE HOLY LAND

I don't regret the experience though, for I guess I'm one of those who would had to have lived through a once-in-a-lifetime event. But, being the deep thinker that I am and always have been,

BETHLEHEM, ENTRANCE TO THE HOLY MANGER

a philosopher by nature who constantly recieves messages and guidance along with inspirations and revelations which influence my daily life, I was not impressed by the man made show, created with such naive understanding - the surface ritual that was meant to commemorate the appearance of a divine personality who had reached the heights of earthly wisdom and awareness, yet chose to return and aid the younger souls who hadn't yet discovered their own divinity. I am probably speaking of things too strange for the present capacity of your understanding, or on a level beyond your own level of consciousness, but don't think that I feel better or more holy than anyone else, it is just that I have been strongly compelled to find answers to profound questions, and have reached this point on the path to self awareness, only with a violent desire to know life, and with diversified always against the futility within my own personality.

Surely most young people ask themselves who they are and what their life is all about—this is a natural part of growing up and goes along with the youthful, idealistic approach to the future, but most people fall into a pit. When they see their surroundings only in terms of earthly reality, and they grow old because of their fear of death and a lack of belief in themselves, faith in eternal realities, understanding of their life's purpose, or awareness of their own potential. I have walked too far to turn back now, knowing enough not to be afraid of where I stand, and I mostly stand alone, watching people create problems for themselves and coping with unnecessary emotions and conflicts, all from a lack of honest communication between their own inner and outer conscience. You see, Christmas to me means not the birth of Jesus to the Virgin Mary so much as the birth of new awareness — the realization of my own Christ Spirit — the spirit that is the sole link between a person and Divine Wisdom, Divine Thought, Divine Mind, or the Eternal Word, these being all just names for one thing—that which most people call God. New discoveries about myself are all the stimulation I really need ("If you know yourself, you know everything") and all I must do is think, listening to my own inner voice instead of outside distractions, so I'm rewarded with new understanding each day, as long as I choose to open my mind and be aware of thoughts, feelings and surroundings in relation to myself. You must think this is very selfish and leaves no room in my actions for sharing and giving, but just the opposite is true. As an understanding and appreciation for my own life grows, so does a concern for the progress and evolution of the self-awareness in others' lives, and I am constantly talking to people who seem to be drawn to me, people who find it easy to relax and open up in my presence. I'm not speaking about just a few experiences, but many of varied durations that have occurred in the last four years, at first confusing and surprising to me, but then quite fulfilling as they kept happening with regularity. Of course, approaching complete strangers for portraits helps in this purpose, and the act of drawing a person's face often breaks down their instinctive defenses. It can be said that I was given this artistic gift for a special reason. Well, I've been writing for a long time, and the half-moon has long since replaced the setting sun. I began by thinking of my concrete surroundings and the new experiences of last night, but the time and place have inspired me enough to reveal things that have been in my mind a long time. Perhaps part of it is the presence of this family who have taken me in as one of their own—a presence which fulfills a need to inhabit this village, and because they have given to me such a precious thing, I must feel a need to give you a precious part of myself also. This book, prepared with so much time and care, is not the real present I give, but it's my thoughts that are the true gift, only because I have never revealed them to you before. I sure hope they don't confuse, intimidate, disgust or anger you in any way, for they've been written out of love, and also appreciation, as I know I would never have reached my present state if I had had different experiences or a different environment.

CANA

Cana tells us something of Jesus' nature. He was so humble that for thirty years He lived in obscurity as the son of a carpenter, fashioning farming implements and delivering them to people's houses. But His authority, grace and majesty are as great as His humility. This becomes evident the moment He steps into the open and begins His public ministry. Jesus needs say but a word and water is transformed into wine — a miracle takes place.

Jesus of Nazareth, a man attested to you by God with mighty works and wonders and signs which God did through him in your midst. Acts 2: 22

Cana proclaims that Jesus is the Lord Almighty, who turns water into wine and who can still today, by one word, transform anything: sorrow into joy, and mountains of difficulties into straight paths. But do we bring our needs to Him?

(text of a plaque in the church — revised translation)

Cana occupies a special place in the hearts of Christians. It was here, seven kilometres northeast of Nazareth, on the road to Tiberias, that Jesus performed his **first miracle** while attending a wedding feast [John 2:1—11].

"Jesus said to them, 'Fill the jars with water'. And they filled them up to the brim. He said to them, 'Now draw some out, and take it to the feast'. So they took it. When the steward of the feast tasted the water now become wine..."

The Franciscans believe that the **Church of the First Miracle of Christ**, which they built in 1881, stands over the site where the wedding feast was held because the crypt, which you may enter, is built around a dried-up well and a large rock with a scooped-out hollow obviously intended for washing.

This church stands over the ruins of a 6th century Byzantine building that was either a church or a synagogue. A mosaic inscription in Aramaic, found here and still displayed beneath a trap-door in the nave, states that the mosaic pavement was made by Jose, son of Tanhum and his sons. The Franciscans hold that Jose may refer to Joseph, Count of Tiberias, a favourite of the Christian-Roman Emperor, Constantine.

A **replica of the wine jars** in use in Christ's time rests above the slab of rock in the crypt.

The Franciscans also supervise the Chapel of St. Bartholomew at the northern end of the village. St. Bartholomew was the Nathanael of the Gospel of St. John and was a native of Cana.

Other churches in this compact little predominantly Christian-Arab village include two supervised by Greek Catholics and Greek Orthodox.

KANA, LOWER GALILEE

TABGHA

Site commemorating the Multiplication of the Loaves and Fishes.

Here Jesus is manifested in His power and glory. Because He is Love, it is His nature to give generously. Thus long ago He took what little there was — five loaves and two fish — and they were multiplied. Thousands ate and were satisfied.

Jesus said, "Bring me the five loaves and two fish." And they all ate and were satisfied. see Matthew 14: 15—21

Jesus, Love incarnate, is constrained to help wherever He sees His children in want and distress. But He waits for empty hands outstretched to Him, wherein He may lay His gifts.

(text of a plaque in the entrance to the Church of the Multiplication of the Loaves and Fishes — revised translation)

CAPERNAUM

Capernaum was the city where Jesus resided. Its inhabitants often heard Him preaching and they witnessed more of His miracles than other people. Why should Capernaum of all places be thrown down to hell (Matthew 11: 23), when its inhabitants enjoyed listening to Jesus and flocked to Him by the thousand? Yes, why? In all their eagerness to hear Jesus' words they failed to repent and turn from all their words, behaviour and deeds that were not good in the eyes of God and the light of His commandments.

Privilege entails responsibility. Revelations, divine favours, such as the experience of God's aid and miracles, oblige us to act upon His word and turn from ways that are not good. Otherwise God will cast the favoured, the exalted from their throne — whereas He raises the lowly, the ones who are far-off. This is what happened to the Roman centurion, who built the synagogue here, who believed Jesus' word and obeyed it.

Capernaum, now leveled to the ground, warns us. "Do not take your words for deeds!" Only he who actually does the will of God will enter the kingdom of heaven. Neither religious experiences, nor the gifts of the Spirit, such as speaking in other tongues, healing or miracle-working, will bring us into the kingdom of heaven — only genuine discipleship, which entails death to self. In other words, we have to make a clean break with sin, sever all earthly bonds and fight a battle of faith even to the point of shedding blood. But whoever does so will attain the crown and the kingdom of heaven.

TABGHA, LAKE OF GALILEE

CAPERNAUM

↑ SEA OF GALILEE AS SEEN FROM THE MOUNT OF BEATITUDES

MOUNT TABOR

The Mount of Transfiguration tells us of the great glory of Jesus. His body was radiant like the sun and even His garments were shining with the splendour of God, which He bore within Him. But this Tabor experience, when the glory of God was revealed, was also marked by the committal to suffering before Jesus went down the path to Jerusalem, the path that would lead to bitter sorrow, the path that would lead to the Cross. From then on Jesus' suffering bore the glory of sublime transfiguration.

Dedication to suffering produces transfiguration and lets the glory of God shine forth. The Tabor experience was to strengthen Jesus — the end of His path of sorrows would also be supreme glory. The hour of Transfiguration on Mount Tabor was the guarantee for this.

And Jesus was transfigured before them; and his face did shine as the sun.   Matthew 17: 2 A.V.

We are changed into the same image from glory to glory.   2 Corinthians 3: 18 A.V.

The hour of Transfiguration came for Jesus when He was about to enter the night of suffering and death. As members of His Body, we can only receive the grace of transfiguration, which He has won for us, by following the same path — the pathway of humiliation and purification.

(text of a plaque at the ruins to the left of the path leading to the Basilica of the Transfiguration — revised translation)

THE GREEK ORTHODOX CONVENT IN BETHANY ↓

BETHANY

Here Jesus reveals Himself to us in His love. As He said to His disciples in His farewell discourses, He loves those who love Him, and makes His dwelling with them. Bethany must have been a special place for Jesus, a place to which the verse from the Psalms applied, "Here I will dwell; for I have desired it" (Psalm 132: 14).

When Jesus was in Jerusalem, He probably stayed with Mary, Martha and Lazarus in Bethany, unable to spend the night in the city because of the plots of the Pharisees. Here in Bethany Jesus found open hearts that loved Him and eagerly awaited Him at all times. Mary laid all else aside; it was of secondary importance to her. When Jesus came, she hastened to Him and devoted herself fully to Him. She was completely captivated by Jesus. She had eyes and ears for Him alone, for Him whom her soul loved. To love Jesus, to hear words of eternal life from His lips meant everything to her. And Jesus would hasten to Bethany, drawn by this love that awaited Him so expectantly. Here were people who sought to show Him kindness with their love. Consequently, Mary, Martha and their brother Lazarus had a special place in Jesus' heart.

One thing is needful: and Mary hath chosen that good part.   Luke 10: 42 A.V.

To-day as in the past, the love of Jesus seeks a refuge where He is lovingly expected and where He can rest. He finds our hearts are filled with distractions — people, work, our own interests. He longs for us to empty our hearts and lovingly receive Him.

(text of a plaque near the entrance to the Franciscan church)

Bethany: Known from the New Testament as the village in which Jesus lodged during his stay in Jerusalem. The home of Martha and Mary, and the site of the miraculous raising of Lazarus from the dead. The miracle is commemorated in the present-day name of the village, el-Azariya, which lies east of the Mount of Olives.

GETHSEMANE —
THE BASILICA OF THE AGONY
(also known as the Church of All Nations)

A huge rock lies before the altar of this church — the Rock of the Agony. At this site we shall find Jesus when we contemplate what took place here long ago.

At this rock the Son of God knelt in the agony of death. Weak as a gentle lamb that is attacked by a ravening beast, He nevertheless fought like a lion against hell, and thus against Satan, Death and sin — even sweating blood. It was a life-and-death struggle. The fate of mankind, His children, whom He dearly loved, was at stake. He yearned to deliver them from Satan.

The words uttered by Jesus during this battle revealed His heart. Not words of mistrust and rebellion against God, but rather deeply moving words came from Jesus' lips in response to all the torment that God let Him undergo. "My Father, not as I will, but as Thou wilt." In childlike trust Jesus surrendered His will to God. This was the weapon with which He defeated the prince of death and emerged from the battle as Victor.

"My Father, if it be possible, let this cup pass from me; nevertheless, not as I will, but as thou wilt."

Matthew 26: 39

O Jesus, in the darkness of night and grief Thou didst utter these words of surrender and trust to God the Father. In gratitude and love I will say with Thee, in my hours of fear and distress, "My Father, I do not understand Thee, but I trust Thee."

(text of a plaque on a rock beneath one of the ancient olive trees in the Garden of Gethsemane — revised translation)

Garden of Gethsemane: The area at the foot of the Mount of Olives is the place to which Jesus retired at the time of his betrayal together with his disciples. The ancient olive trees which grow on this section of the hillside explain the name, derived from the Hebrew, "Gat Shemen" — oil press.

JERUSALEM, GARDEN OF GETHSEMANE

One of the most aesthetically enchanting churches in the Holy Land stands at the foot of the Mt. of Olives over the site where Jesus Christ prayed shortly before being arrested.

Its official name is the Basilica of the Agony. But as donations came from many countries for the building of the present church in 1924, it has become widely known as the Church of all Nations.

It is built within the Garden of Gethsemane where eight of the trees, still bearing olives, are believed by scientists to be more than 2,000 years old.

The focal point of the interior of the church is a slab of rock before the altar. It was cut during the time of the Emperor Theodosius, about 380 C.E., for the first church built on this sacred site.

When the Persians ransacked Jerusalem in 614 C.E. the church was one of the first holy places to be destroyed. During the centuries that followed successive churches were rebuilt and destroyed on the same site.

The arrival of the Crusaders gave the native Christians a period of protection and they erected a small chapel over the ruins of the churches. This was later enlarged and called St. Saviour's.

Saladin's forces wrecked this church and it was only in 1666 that the Franciscans — current custodians of the Church of all Nations — regained possession of the ruins and the adjacent Garden of Gethsemane.

The present church has six columns supporting 12 cupolas on which the coats of arms of all the donor-nations can be seen.

One of the most entrancing aspects of the interior is the soft orange and mauve colours that come from the translucent, alabaster stained glass windows. The serene and contemplative mood for the worshipper is enhanced by these colours infiltrating into an otherwise darkened church.

Near the church is the Grotto of the Agony — an underground shrine that marks the location where Jesus was arrested.

THE VALLEY OF KIDRON

The vale of tears! Once David, with a large crowd of subjects, passed through this valley shedding tears — cast out of Jerusalem by his own son. About one thousand years later Jesus passed through this valley, but unaccompanied by any followers. His disciples had deserted Him. He did not go as a free man like David; rather He was led in chains. He was driven through the Kidron Valley like a beast to the slaughter under the cruel hands of the guards who led Him to the judges.

From the Holy Bible.

And all the country wept with a loud voice, and all the people passed over: the king also himself passed over the brook Kidron, and all the people passed over, toward the way of the wilderness.

II Samuel 15,23

At the same time Jesus spoke to the crowd. "Do you take me for a bandit", he said, "that you have come out with swords and cudgels to arrest me?" Day after day I sat teaching in the temple, and you did not lay hands on me. But this has all happened to fulfil what the prophets wrote."

Then the disciples all deserted him and ran away.

The troops with their commander, and the Jewish police, now arrested Jesus and secured him.

From Matth. 26 and John 18

THE VIA DOLOROSA

On this street we can see Jesus in spirit before us on His way to Calvary. Silently, patiently, like a lamb, He bears the Cross, staggering beneath its heavy weight as He passes through the noisy, crowded, narrow streets of Jerusalem.

And he bearing his cross went forth into a place called the place of a skull, which is called in the Hebrew Golgotha. John 19: 17 A.V.

Whoever belongs to Jesus cannot but follow the path He took, for love is constrained to accompany Jesus on the way of the cross.

(text of a plaque at the chapel of the seventh station — revised translation)

Via Dolorosa: The winding stepped street which marks the way of the Cross leads through the Old City from the tower of Antonia, near St. Stephen's Gate, to the Holy Sepulchre. Arched over at several points, and always marked by an oriental character, the Via Dolorosa is divided into fourteen stations, marking episodes on Jesus' route to Calvary. Nine stations are recorded outside the Church of the Holy Sepulchre, the last five being inside the church. Pilgrims may join the Franciscan Fathers procession along the Via Dolorosa every Friday at 3 p.m., starting from the tower of Antonia, just inside St. Stephen's Gate.

THE CHURCH OF ST. PETER IN GALLICANTU

In the hour of the denial Jesus' sad gaze falls upon His disciple Peter — and in this response to the disciple's disgraceful behaviour we discover Jesus' heart. Jesus turns to Peter, who has inflicted such suffering upon Him. He does not reject him, nor does He give up hope for him. He simply looks at him in unspeakable grief. And this loving, sorrowful gaze of Jesus has power; Peter comes to repentance. He becomes a new man, one that loves Jesus; for love is born of repentance. Such repentance is willing to suffer anything, as Peter later proved when he was even prepared to be crucified.

The Lord turned and looked at Peter. And he went out and wept bitterly. Luke 22: 61f.

Jesus, once filled with sorrow because of Peter's sin, is now gazing at us. He longs that we too might shed tears of repentance over our sins. The more we weep in contrition for having grieved Jesus, the more fervent our love for Him will be.

(text of a plaque at the Scala Santa — revised translation)

St. Peter in Gallicantu: The church which stands on the eastern slope of Mount Zion marks the presumed site of the home of the high priest Caiaphas, where Peter denied Jesus ("before the cock crows twice, thou shalt deny me thrice" — Gallicante means cockcrow). A modern assumptionist foundation, the church stands over a number of interesting remains.

THE VIA DOLOROSA ⇨

THE TOMB OF CHRIST

Here we find Jesus as the One whom the grave could not hold and who was stronger than hell and Death. Jesus emerged from the gloomy grave as the Prince of Victory. The Crucified Lord is now the Risen Lord. The foe Satan is vanquished. And from now on, in spite of the raging of the powers of darkness and all the Enemy's attacks, Jesus goes forth from victory unto victory. First in His fold, the host of true believers. Then after His second coming He will triumphantly establish His rule over the nations. And in the end as Victor over the entire world and universe He will bring forth a new world, where righteousness will reign.

Holy Sepulchre: In the very heart of the Old City is the shrine most sacred to Christianity — the magnificent church which marks the site of the crucifixion, burial and resurrection of Jesus. Situated on the hill known as Golgotha (Calvaria in Latin, whence Calvary), the present church is essentially a Crusader structure, though it has undergone many additions and modifications (a substantial restoration programme has been underway for some time, and the building is currently under scaffolding). The five last stations of the Via Dolorosa are situated inside the church, authority over which is divided between various Christian congregations.

COMPOUND OF THE HOLY SEPULCHRE ⇩

THE ELEONA GROTTO on the Mount of Olives

Site of the Ascension and Jesus' Eschatological Discourses.

How can I find Jesus at this site? By believing His words about His second coming. Here on the Mount of Olives, from where Jesus ascended to heaven, He prophesied that He would come again in power and glory (Matthew 24 & 25). According to His word this event will take place in a specific age, when the signs of the end times are being fulfilled — for instance, when His faithful ones are hated and persecuted by all nations, and lawlessness gains the upper hand. And in our day it has come true that mankind lives almost entirely detached from the commandments and ordinances of God, in the sins of sodomy, violence and criminality. In this century the persecution of Christians is more prevalent than in all previous centuries and is threatening to become universal. Jesus said: "When you see all these things, you know that he [the Son-of-man] is near, at the very gates" (Matthew 24: 33).

This same Jesus, which is taken up from you into heaven, shall so come in like manner as ye have seen him go into heaven. Acts 1: 11 b. A.V.

When the trumpet call sounds at midnight, only those whose hearts are tuned to the sound will hear it. They are people who love Jesus and wait expectantly for Him.

Mount of Olives: The hill to the east of the Old City is known as the Mount of Olives. For countless centuries it has been the site of Jewish burials, and many are the Jews whose last wish it was, wherever they were scattered throughout the diaspora, to be buried on this spot, the nearest point to the holy city where burial was permitted. The tradition springs from a belief that it is from here that the Messiah will enter Jerusalem, bringing about a resurrection of the dead. The majority of the Jewish tombstones of the area were desecrated by the Jordanian army, though restoration work is now proceeding. In Christian tradition the Mount is the site of Jesus' ascension.

*Yes, he whom Easter joy sets free
His heart cries out his Lord to see,
Though Satan loud may threaten.
My thankful heart the Victor knows,
Hails Jesus, Lord of all His foes,
For Jesus is the Victor!
For Christ, our Lord, is risen!*

CHAPEL OF THE ASCENSION ON THE MOUNT OF OLIVES

Jerusalem

The Garden Tomb

Jan. 31st (Sat.) 13th hour ~ All this talk about Jesus makes me very sad, for the Christians, thinking they are the chosen ones to be saved on the "Judgement Day," are missing the whole point as to what their Savior was trying to tell them. Jesus told his disciples to become "fishers of men," and through the generations, that's just what the masses misguidingly complied with: they were like schools of fish, or flocks of sheep following their "Good Shepherd." They bowed down before their One Messiah, begging for his goodness and mercy, worshipping his actions, his style. They became attached to his words, memorized them and repeated them countlessly, but the people never really understood the true meaning behind them. Jesus was a seeker of truth - a thinker, and when he realized those truths which took 30 years to formulate, he of course desired to share them, thus beginning his ministry. Christians do not realize it but the teachings of their Master dwell greatly on the importance of the body, and how one abuses it or reveres it. He himself fasted for 40 days as did Moses and Elijah, in order to rid the body of a lifetime of poisons, and recieve divine revelations, before he set out to teach the people. This period of abstinence was not done far away in nature, for that would have been too easy. Besides, "Satan" dwells in the midst of corrupt society, attracted to people with impure thoughts and ways. To be tempted by the "Devil," Jesus had to walk through the "poisonous" market streets where dwelled the clothes and jewelry merchants, prostitutes, food vendors, money changers and drug pushers - the life that the majority of us are so attached to. He passed through this maze but wasn't attracted by it because he saw its futility, hopelessness, confusion, ugliness and mortality. Such a world could only cause pain, suffering and an early death, for both the body and the mind. Jesus learned to live with only the necessities - the more possessions one has, the more one worries about them. Why throw away so much energy building up an impressive surface when the most treasured possession is peace of mind? The one material thing that we have been blessed with is our body - our temple; the House of God. How can it be the House of God? Because we are created with love, a divine spark dwells within us. It is the "Christ Spirit," our link to the "Creator," and because all of us have it, we are all in the same "family"- brothers and sisters, right? That's why Jesus said that only through him could one reach God. The Bible is filled with symbolism. But how do we reach that pure part within us? Simply by becomming as children - by not eating the fruit of the tree of the knowledge of good and evil; in other words, not judging what's right and wrong. The experiences we term good are those that boost our ego and

give momentary pleasure, but those we term bad, are the mis-
takes that teach us most about ourselves. Do we ever learn to be more
honest or self appreciative? Rarely. Children start off by taking
only what they need, until they are taught selfishness and gluttony.
The little ones are not shown the purpose of the things around them,
and then when they use something for other than its purpose, their
elders tell them that their action is bad. So often children ask
"why", but the only answer they get is, "because I said so." Live
simply; live naturally; live as a child in awe of the beauty surrounding you. Just open yourselves and take the gifts that are
waiting. Disregard the hell and seek the heaven within your own
mind. You must learn to love yourself; marvel at your own divinity,
your own life's purpose. Do not let the empure life tempt or distract
you, for you must be the master of your kingdom. And
finally, keep your temple clean and pure. Take care of how you
nourish your body, and resist the drugs and empty calorie junk
foods that poison it and make you weak. The natural way to health
is through fasting. All animals instinctively fast when they're sick.
Digesting foods, especially the concoctions people dump into their
stomachs these days, takes great amounts of the body's energy, so just
as we rest our muscles, why not rest our digestive tract - give
our internal selves a good housecleaning. This is usually done in
25 days before the body begins to eat its own protein. All kinds of
ailments like asthma, arthritis, liver problems, bursitis, balding,
skin problems etc. can be cured by your internal doctor. Besides
losing weight the quickest way possible and the easiest because
one isn't hungry (any food awakens the appetite and brings back the
memory of the last meal) one becomes more relaxed, with a brighter
outlook on life. Today is the 14th day of my first long fast, and
I shall continue until my tongue becomes clean and my appetite returns. The wart on my foot that still gave me pain after
countless trips to the doctor, is almost gone after 2 weeks, and
the scar on my arm is less bumpy! Of course one should eat
the right foods to break the fast, then continue on a primitive
diet, which is the best one. One of the ironies of civilization
is that the meals which take the longest to prepare, are the
most destructive, causing internal blockage and excess
mucus which are perfect homes for disease - causing or-
ganisms. Remember that the fall of man occured when
he left the Garden and settled down to cultivate wheat
for bread, used fire to cook his food, and domesticated
animals, thus causing himself disease and pain in childbirth.
Soon after came the first death by the hand of another human being.

THE ULTIMATE DIET FOR YOUTH, BEAUTY, HEALTH, PEACE AND OBESITY

8 AM ~ Drink one pint water, two pints cider vinegar, honey to sweeten.
7:30 to 8 ~ Drink 2 to 3 cups herbal tea (camomile, rosehips) with honey
9:30 to 10 ~ Eat the first solid food to be taken in the day:
  Start with one raw apple with the skin, sometimes another fruit.
  Eat one cup of plain yogurt with honey, or a boiled egg, never fried.
12 to 1 ~ Eat a small meal to cleanse, preventing constipation:
  One cup of raw, natural wheat bran from a bakery or health store.
  Two tablespoons of raw, uncooked sesame seeds for calcium.
  Mix this with enough water to soften and honey to sweeten.
  Then add one very ripe banana (almost black) chopped up.
3 to 4 PM ~ Should be the main, heavy meal of the day but if events
  forbid it, exchange it for the snack at 9 PM. Here's the main meal:
  Fish, never fried (Sardines with the bones are the healthiest) or 1 egg.
  One whole lemon with the pulp as well as the juice, for the fish.
  Parsley or similar raw greens, and eat a lot for the fiber.
  One cup of boiled soy beans (best) kidney beans or peas.
  (Can substitute one medium baked or boiled potato with the skin.)
  Half of a clove of garlick should be boiled with the beans and eaten.
  One medium raw carrot with the skin as a "vitamin A" source.
  One small raw beet with the skin – eaten three times weekly.
  One avacado or some olives add an extra source of protein.
  Raw green pepper and onions can be added for taste.
  Drink a glass of water before meal 3 to 4 cups of Brandy during, if wanted
7 to 8 PM ~ Eat no solid foods after this and before going to bed.
  One cup of raw, unsalted nuts, to provide protein and oil.
  (The best nuts are almonds, brazil, peanuts and roasted chestnuts)
  Eat 8 dried dates to cut the oil and provide lots of iron.
  Eat one handful of unsalted sunflower seeds.
During the evening drink some herbal tea (catnip) with honey.
Before retiring take two tablespoons of pure olive oil (to cleanse.)
An extremely important reminder: After each bite, put your
  fork or spoon down and chew well and long enough for the food
  to liquefy in your mouth. If not, the food isn't digested well.
In between meals, drink only water or pure grape juice.
Don't eat fruits and vegetables at the same meal.
Don't eat dairy products except for yogurt, which aids digestion.
Never take any forms of drugs, which includes:
  Sugar ~ a processed chemical of no food value at all.
  Bread, pasta, white rice – dead food, stripped of original value.
  Doctors medicin ~ poison which is stored, not digested.
  Cooked foods except the ones I've mentioned.
Stick closely to this diet, neither adding or taking away from it.

BREAKING A LONG FAST

1st DAY ~ Eat 1 orange section every 10 min. starting at 7 AM.
Eat 1 whole orange every 3 hrs ~at 10 AM, 1 PM, 4 PM and 7 PM.
Drink as much water as possible all day.

2nd DAY ~ Eat 1 orange every 3 hrs. starting at 7 AM, ending at 7 PM.
Eat 1 apple at 9 AM, 1 banana at 1 PM and 3 PM, 4 dates at 5 PM.
Drink as much water as possible all day.

3rd DAY ~ Eat 1 orange every 3 hrs starting at 7 AM, ending at 7 PM.
add 2 tbs. yogurt to meals of apple, bananas and dates of 2nd day.
Drink as much water as possible all day.

4th DAY ~ Eat 1 orange every 3 hrs starting at 7 AM ending at 7 PM.
add 2 tbs wheat bran with honey to each meal with the yogurt.
Drink as much water as possible all day.

5th DAY ~ Eat 1 orange every 3 hrs starting at 7 AM, ending at 7 PM.
add 2 tbs. nuts to each meal with the honey, yogurt & wheat bran.
Drink as much water as possible all day.

6th DAY ~ Awake and drink some herbal tea with honey.
9 AM ~ Eat 1 apple, 1 cup of plain yogurt and some honey.
Noon ~ Eat 1 cup wheat bran, 2 tbs. sesame seeds, 1 banana, honey.
3 PM ~ Eat 1 cup beans, garlick, chopped parsley, 1 carrot, olives.
6 PM ~ Eat 1 cup of nuts, 8 dried dates and sunflower seeds.
9 PM ~ Drink some herbal tea and honey.
Before retiring take 2 tbs. of pure olive oil.

7th DAY ~ Awake and drink water, vinegar and honey.
8 AM ~ Drink some herbal tea with honey.
9 AM ~ Eat 1 apple and 1 boiled egg.
Noon ~ Eat 1 cup wheat bran, sesame seeds, 1 banana, honey.
3 PM ~ 1 boiled egg, 1 cup beans w/ garlick, parsley, carrot, olives.
6 PM ~ Eat 1 cup of nuts, 8 dried dates, and sunflower seeds.
9 PM ~ Drink some herbal tea and honey.
Before retiring take 2 tbs. of pure olive oil.

8th DAY ~ Eat normally except for the Brandy.

BREAKING A SHORT FAST

1st DAY ~ Same as the first day in the list above.
2nd DAY ~ Same as the third day in the list above.
3rd DAY ~ Same as the fifth day in the list above.
4th DAY ~ Same as the sixth day in the list above.
5th DAY ~ Same as the seventh day in the list above.
6th DAY ~ Eat normally except for the Brandy.

Eldridge Cleaver:
Arabs are racists

By WOLF BLITZER
Jerusalem Post Correspondent

WASHINGTON. — Eldridge Cleaver, the former U.S. exile who recently returned to the U.S. and is now in a California prison awaiting trial, has bitterly accused the Arab people of being "amongst the most racist people on earth."

Cleaver, who spent several years in Algeria, condemned the campaign to equate Zionism with racism, declaring that "Jews have not only suffered particularly from racist persecution, they have done more than any other people in history to expose and condemn racism."

The Jerusalem Post has obtained a copy of Cleaver's statement on Zionism and Arab racism, which has not yet been published in America. Because of Cleaver's reputation as a leading Black radical, his remarks on the subject are expected to receive wide publicity. The following is the full text:

Two aspects of the recent UN resolution labelling Zionism as racist both shocked and surprised me. Shocked because of all the people in the world, the Jews have not only suffered particularly from racist persecution, they have done more than any other people in history to expose and condemn racism. Generations of Jewish social scientists and scholars have laboured long and hard in every field of knowledge, from anthropology to psychology, to lay bare and refute all claims of racial inferiority and superiority. To condemn the Jewish survival doctrine of Zionism as racism, is a travesty upon the truth.

Secondly, I am surprised that the Arabs would choose to establish a precedent condemning racism because it can so easily and righteously be turned against them. Having lived intimately for several years amongst the Arabs, I know them to be amongst the most racist people on earth. This is particularly true of their attitude towards Black people. No one knows this better than Black Africans living along the edges of the Sahara.

Once while travelling through Bamako, Mali, the cab driver flew into a rage when we asked him to take us to the Algerian Embassy. When he learned that we actually lived in Algeria, he concluded that we were crazy. "Man," he said irritatedly, "don't you know that the Arabs still have black slaves?" He was right, although I didn't find it out until later. Many Arab families that can afford to, keep one or two black slaves to do their menial labour. Sometimes they own an entire family. I have seen such slaves with my own eyes. Once I pressed an Algerian official for an explanation of the status of these people, and he ended up describing a complicated form of indentured servitude. The conversation broke up when I told him that it was nothing but a hypocritical form of slavery.

I have the deepest sympathy for the Palestinian people in their search for justice, but I see no net gain for freedom and human dignity in the world of power blocs, because of their ability to underwrite sagging economies for a season, are able to ram through the UN resolutions repugnant to human reason and historical fact.

The combination of Communist dictatorship, theocratic Arab dictatorships, and economically dependent Black African dictatorships are basically united in their opposition to the democratic forces inside their own borders. This gives them a lot in common and loss of room and motivation to wheel and deal amongst themselves. But it is not a combination deserving of respect by people from countries enjoying democratic liberties and traditions of freedom. It is a combination that must be struggled against.

But it seems to me that the Western democracies, the United States above all, are so guilt-ridden because of their past history as colonizers that they now swallow hook, line, and sinker, every half-baked argument emanating from the wise men of the General Assembly.

I believe that the time has come to reexamine the credentials of all the members of the General Assembly. Why should all those little so-called countries with minuscule populations have a vote equal in weight to that of the United States? When such votes are cast in the wreckless manner of the anti-Zionist resolution, it is time to sit up and take notice.

The so-called hard line adopted at the UN by Ambassador Moynihan seems too soft to me, and the support which he is getting in certain political circles is softer still. But the stakes in the struggle in the international arena are high. The General Assembly is no longer filled with Mahatma Gandhis pleading the case of the downtrodden colonized masses. It is now a forum for crude hired killers like Idi Amin Dada, the hatchet man of Uganda.

But it is not enough to criticise the negative aspects of the UN in print and fiery speeches, and then lose the crucial votes when the chips are down. Concrete steps must be taken to render the UN structurally incapable of cynical manipulation by hypocritical power blocs that devour freedom in the name of a just cause and undermine democratic principles with a wreckless distortion of the right to vote.

It may seem paradoxical that I write these words from a prison cell in California. I am certainly not a stranger to racism — I have personally experienced it in the ghettoes and prison yards of America. But I have also personally shared the experience of thousands of men and women now languishing in the prisons of Communist and Third World countries. The cause of democracy and freedom can best be served when men and women speak out against the forces that seek to nullify them, even if this means speaking out from a prison cell.

Golda denies she ignored the Palestinian issue

Jerusalem Post Staff

WASHINGTON. — Former Prime Minister Golda Meir denied Wednesday that she disregards the importance of solving the Palestinian problem, a charge she has often been accused of during recent years.

In an article published in the "New York Times," Mrs. Meir insisted that there is no room for speculation regarding Israel's position on the PLO if the terrorist organization should accept Israel's right to exist. But, she continued, "This does not mean that at this stage I disregard whatever national aspirations Palestinian Arabs have developed in recent years."

Claiming that she has been regularly misquoted regarding her controversial statement made several years ago that "there is no Palestinian people," Mrs. Meir said that the rest of that statement did affirm that "there are Palestinian refugees."

Mrs. Meir is currently in London on a short private visit. At a lunch in her honour, attended by British Foreign Secretary James Callaghan, Liberal Party leader Jeremy Thorpe, British political and trade union leaders and prominent Jewish personalities, she said that "If anyone fought against the idea of Palestine and the idea of a Palestinian people it was the Arabs." She recalled that in 1966 PLO leader Ahmed Shukeiri had said there was never such a thing as Palestine — it was Southern Syria.

Feb. 15th (Sun) 15th hour ~
These are just some words
I cut out of the "Jerusalem
Post", a pro-Jewish paper I
pick up every Sabbath Eve
(Friday) for its English
content and supplement on
that day. I'm not very
politically opinionated,
looking at civilization in
terms of its general evolution from different stages
advancing towards a
spiritual end. Wars, bru-
tality, separate nations,
slavery and oppression are
all in our history, but we are
slowly coming away from
these things simply by being aware of their destructive nature. We live more
honestly, question hypo-
crisy, challenge authority,
demand our rights, fight
for acceptance, and the

STAMP COLUMN / Harvey D. Wolinetz

Arab refugee stamps

This is the first of a regular series on stamps of the world.

ONE OF THE MAJOR themes of Arab propaganda assault against Israel in the philatelic as in the political field has been the Palestine refugees.

In 1960, while the Palestinian refugees of the West Bank and the Gaza Strip were under Jordanian and Egyptian control respectively, Egypt, Syria and Yemen each issued a similar set of stamps showing wretched-looking refugees pointing at a map of Palestine from behind a barbed wire fence. The Arabs were clearly stating that the West Bank and Gaza Strip were not sufficient to solve the refugee problem. They needed all of Israel's lands too.

Between 1948 and 1967 most of the Palestine refugees lived in the Gaza Strip and West Bank. Both Egypt and Jordan treated these lands as occupied territories and never as integral parts of their respective countries. They even issued special stamps (or overprinted their regular issues) carrying the name Palestine for use in these occupied areas.

THE REFUGEES themselves were treated as a conquered people by their Arab brothers in Egypt and Jordan. They were not accorded citizenship or even the rights of citizens. The Gaza Strip occupants were confined to that area and were not allowed to travel even to Egypt. Although the West Bank inhabitants were permitted to travel, they were prohibited from establishing businesses and factories and were kept chained to their poverty.

Exploiting the refugees as a political instrument against Israel, the Arab States never made any ef-

1970 Egyptian stamp

fort to relieve their plight. The refugee problem was used to motivate hatred and terrorism along Israel's frontiers and to put forth Arab claims to all of Palestine.

Since the Six Day War, when Israel established control over the Gaza Strip and West Bank areas, the economic and cultural standards of the Palestinians has been dramatically improved. This has not prevented Egypt from issuing a stamp every year depicting the same wretched refugees. The 1970 stamp showed armed men leading the refugees towards a map of Palestine.

Even the latest interim agreement with Egypt has been ignored to the extent that Egypt has continued its anti-Israel propaganda with another stamp showing the refugees behind a barbed wire fence. The stamp also makes reference to Arafat's United Nations speech by showing a rifle and olive branch around a picture of the United Nations building.

fact is that at this point in time, we are getting results. This "age of
Truth" that is dawning cannot be denied. A Moroccan family I
lived with had two very young black girls to do the menial jobs. I
wouldn't call them slaves, but whatever this lot, it's not really important. I'm now living with a Palestinian family, so am aware of the
injustices done to them, but these so-called "atrocities" are not so
important either. People must dare to accept what they have, for
all that they "possess" in their life, is only
lent to them, for a teaching purpose.
The only things that are really
important are eternal. Last
Tuesday when it snowed, the Jews
took over the Mosque of Omar, the
only thing left that the Arabs could
call their own. Ignorance is
man's only enemy, and what
a man gives to his neighbor, is
returned to him tenfold. *

OLIVE
SPRIG

Feb. 17th (Tuesday) 17th hour ~ I have spent some peaceful hours in solitude during the last few days, contemplating my time in this country, especially the two weeks I have lived in this old house in the Christian Quarter of "The Golden City", Jerusalem. Jacob's mother and brother Nabil, who are the only ones living here now, are visiting Nadia, his sister, so I am left alone this afternoon, happy in the silence that allows me to write this last entry to my book. I'm sitting at the table in the main room next to the kitchen. This room is where the two of them eat, sleep, watch television and gather with the rest of the family, which includes Jacob's three sisters, Nadia, Helen and Nelli, and their husbands Victor, Fouad and Alfred. A fourth sister Katie, whom I have never met, lives with her husband Johnnie, in Nazareth. Last Saturday evening I had the three couples over for supper, as I am flying to Athens tomorrow. It had been less than a week since I broke my three week long fast, the last week of which I had spent painting Jacob's old room on the rooftop, in preparation for taking it over. Nabil, 28 years old, but mentally about twelve, due to a sickness at the age of four, was a great deal of help to me, but because of the paint fumes, I had to sleep in the main room with him and his mother. I had wanted to liven up the pastel green, plaster-cracked walls in this room also, but they shall have to remain just about the same as they have been for the 600 to 700 years since this old stone house was erected, (with much care I may add, as evidenced in the arched ceilings of each room) Downstairs on the street level is the foundation of an early Christian church, which is nothing but a hole in the dirt which the family has used for dumping rubbage. The metal front door, so small I have to duck through, is painted light blue, and because it is surrounded during the day by hanging dresses from the souvenir shop next door, I sometimes overlook it. When I use my key to enter and leave each day, it gives me a good feeling to know I have a home on such a colorful, historical old street, where families have lived in the same houses for generations. This door, I so frequently use is right up a few steps from the VIII - station on the Via Dolorosa, the place where

Jesus met the city women. Every morning A leave to take a shower at Nadia's house outside the walls, for there's no hot water here, and A walk down the narrow stone way to the main market street that leads to Damascus Gate, and divides the Christian and

THE OLD CITY OF JERUSALEM

Jerusalem is a city which offers so much for the visitor that it's difficult to know where to begin. The amount of detail and information provided often proves mind-boggling for the tourist whose time is limited. The highlight of highlights is, of course, the Old City, which contains some of the holiest sanctuaries of Christianity, Judaism and Islam.

Surrounded by walls which stretch for a distance of 4 kilometres and enclose the area of about 20 acres, the Old City has eight gates (7 open) and consists of four areas — the QUARTERS.

The Jewish Quarter is in the southern section of the city. Largely destroyed by the Arabs in 1949 it is now being rebuilt. Interesting to visit are the ruins of the Ramban Synagogue (see opposite page), and other places of worship.

The Armenian Quarter is in the western section, between the Jaffa and Zion Gates. It is populated by Armenians whose forebears came to the country from the 5th century onwards. Examples of Armenian art can be found in the beautiful Church of St. James which dominates the Quarter.

The Christian Quarter lies in the north-western section from the Jaffa and Damascus Gates. Populated by Christians of various denominations, it contains many holy shrines — the most important being the Holy Sepulchre.

The largest of the Quarters, located in the central and north-eastern section, is the Moslem Quarter. The Via Dolorosa cuts across this.

Other places of interest in the Old City are the Temple Mount (Mount Moriah), the Western Wall, the Citadel and David's Tower. All steeped in religious and historical significance.

Moslem Quarters. Such an exciting walk this is! Tourists crowd the covered street, blocking the way for Arab boys pushing carts and leading donkeys carrying crates of vegetables and fruits, or large tin cans of gas. Shop-owners stand just inside their doorways, ready to sell everything from plastic kitchenware, postcards, portable gas burners and shish-kebabs. Neighborhood women doing their morning marketing usually stay clear of this place and go to the cheaper streets off to the side where they can buy fresh eggs, just plucked poultry and newly-slaughtered goats and sheep. The heads, feet and all, the innards are put out on the tables and strung up on hooks along with the choicer cuts, and one doesn't find many squeamish foreigners around there. A often walk that way just so A can go faster, and not have to dodge people. The locals know me by now and A'm not so harrassed as A was in the beginning, except the young boys always enjoy making comments or bumping my arm as A pass. A had seen all of the sites A cared to see in the Old City, but wanted very much to walk up to the Mount of Olives to view all of it from a distance, so on Sunday A did just that, and took the olive twig that's pasted on one of the preceding pages. As A walked along the ridge at the top, A heard a call to prayer from a nearby mosque and the cry, a different, more haunting one than

Jerusalem. Basilica and Gardens of Gethsemane

meat, as it echoed in the valley on the other side, made me realize for the first time that I would miss this part of the world — its mixture of cultures and religions, and exotic life that constantly stimulates all my senses. I sat on the roof under the full moon the other night, thinking about leaving, and the new experiences that lie ahead as I make my way to the British Isles where I plan on spending the summer. I didn't make the financial gains I had planned for, but the rewards of these two months in Jerusalem drown out any disappointments I may have concerning lack of funds. I've definitely gotten more from this visit that was originally just to spend Christmas in the Holy Land. Well, Nabil and Mrs. Jouzy are now back and the T.V. is on as it always is in the evening, when it makes a blue glow in the tiny window when seen from the dark, quiet street below, evidence that this household is the only one with the noisy contraption, a neighborhood status symbol. This week I saw fighting and stone-throwing in the sacred streets and one afternoon I was lucky to get home safely, as the Arabs rioting because of the mosque takeover, were quieted by teargas. Many days looked upon the city with sad understanding as I have, wondering whether it shall ever truly deserve its name, "City of Peace."

"While you live, your troubles are many, poor Jerusalem, but before your die, you only have to die."
No answer liveth

Printed in the United States
by Baker & Taylor Publisher Services